TEACHER'S PET PUBLICATIONS

LITPLAN TEACHER PACK
for
Tangerine
based on the book by
Edward Bloor

Written by
Christina Stone

© 2008 Teacher's Pet Publications
All Rights Reserved

Copyright Teacher's Pet Publications 2008

Only the student materials in this unit plan (such as worksheets, study questions, and tests) may be reproduced multiple times for use in the purchaser's classroom.

For any additional copyright questions, contact Teacher's Pet Publications.

www.tpet.com

TABLE OF CONTENTS - *Tangerine*

Introduction	5
Unit Objectives	7
Reading Assignment Sheet	8
Unit Outline	9
Study Questions (Short Answer)	13
Quiz/Study Questions (Multiple Choice)	26
Pre-reading Vocabulary Worksheets	57
Lesson One (Introductory Lesson)	79
Non-fiction Assignment Sheet	95
Oral Reading Evaluation Form	87
Writing Assignment 1	91
Writing Assignment 2	99
Writing Assignment 3	107
Writing Evaluation Form	92
Vocabulary Review Activities	120
Extra Writing Assignments/Discussion ?s	109
Unit Review Activities	121
Unit Tests	127
Unit Resource Materials	191
Vocabulary Resource Materials	212

ABOUT THE AUTHOR

Edward Bloor

Edward Bloor was born in Trenton, New Jersey and was an avid soccer player. He grew up in an area where cultural pride was often conveyed through victories in soccer and therefore realized how important sports could be in the lives of people. He played on a great soccer team in high school--but a horrible team while attending college at Fordham University in New York.

He later moved to Orlando, Florida and worked as an English teacher there for three years. His teaching position helped open other job opportunities, leading him to work for Harcourt Brace School Publishers as a senior editor.

During his time as an editor of young adult novels, Bloor decided to try writing a novel of his own. While driving to work each day and watching as Florida's natural environment was slowly destroyed to make way for expensive housing developments, he decided to write a novel examining the lives of those who had once used the land and those who were beginning to use it now. He also brought in his love of soccer, creating his first novel, *Tangerine*.

Since then, Bloor has published *Crusader, Story Time, London Calling*, and *Taken*.

Aside from writing, Bloor enjoys spending time with his wife and two children.

INTRODUCTION *Tangerine*

This LitPlan has been designed to develop students' reading, writing, thinking, and language skills through exercises and activities related to *Tangerine*. It includes twenty lessons, supported by extra resource materials.

The **introductory lesson** introduces students to mysteries. Following the introductory activity, students are given a transition to explain how the activity relates to the book they are about to read. Following the transition, students are given the materials they will be using during the unit. At the end of the lesson, students begin the pre-reading work for the first reading assignment.

The **reading assignments** are approximately thirty pages each; some are a little shorter while others are a little longer. Students have approximately 15 minutes of pre-reading work to do prior to each reading assignment. This pre-reading work involves reviewing the study questions for the assignment and doing some vocabulary work for selected vocabulary words they will encounter in their reading.

The **study guide questions** are fact-based questions; students can find the answers to these questions right in the text. These questions come in two formats: short answer or multiple choice. The best use of these materials is probably to use the short answer version of the questions as study guides for students (since answers will be more complete), and to use the multiple choice version for occasional quizzes.

The **vocabulary work** is intended to enrich students' vocabularies as well as to aid in the students' understanding of the book. Prior to each reading assignment, students will complete a two-part worksheet for selected vocabulary words in the upcoming reading assignment. Part I focuses on students' use of general knowledge and contextual clues by giving the sentence in which the word appears in the text. Students are then to write down what they think the words mean based on the words' usage. Part II nails down the definitions of the words by giving students dictionary definitions of the words and having students match the words to the correct definitions based on the words' contextual usage. Students should then have an understanding of the words when they meet them in the text.

After each reading assignment, students will go back and formulate answers for the study guide questions. Discussion of these questions serves as a **review** of the most important events and ideas presented in the reading assignments.

After students complete reading the work, there is a **vocabulary review** lesson which pulls together all of the fragmented vocabulary lists for the reading assignments and gives students a review of all of the words they have studied.

Following the vocabulary review, a lesson is devoted to the **extra discussion questions/writing assignments**. These questions focus on interpretation, critical analysis, and personal response, employing a variety of thinking skills and adding to the students' understanding of the novel.

There is an **individual project** in this unit. This project requires students to conduct research on the role an environment plays in the lives of the people living in it.

There are three **writing assignments** in this unit, each with the purpose of informing, persuading, or having students express personal opinions. The first writing assignment asks students to persuade a coach to allow an athlete with a physical disability to play on the team. The second writing assignment allows students to solve a crime scene mystery and creatively outline the details of the crime. The third writing assignment gives students several roles from which to write.

There is a non-fiction **reading assignment**. Students must read non-fiction articles, books, etc. to gather information about their themes in our world today.

The **review lesson** pulls together all of the aspects of the unit. The teacher is given four or five choices of activities or games to use which all serve the same basic function of reviewing all of the information presented in the unit.

The **unit test** comes in two formats: multiple choice or short answer. As a convenience, two different tests for each format have been included. There is also an advanced short answer unit test for advanced students.

There are additional **support materials** included with this unit. The **Unit Resource Materials** section includes suggestions for an in-class library, crossword and word search puzzles related to the novel, and extra worksheets. There is a list of **bulletin board ideas** which gives the teacher suggestions for bulletin boards to go along with this unit. In addition, there is a list of **extra class activities** the teacher could choose from to enhance the unit or as a substitution for an exercise the teacher might feel is inappropriate for his/her class. **Answer keys** are located directly after the **reproducible student materials** throughout the unit. The **Vocabulary Resource Materials** section includes similar worksheets and games to reinforce the vocabulary words.

The **level** of this unit can be varied depending upon the criteria on which the individual assignments are graded, the teacher's expectations of his/her students in class discussions, and the formats chosen for the study guides, quizzes and test. If teachers have other ideas/activities they wish to use, they can usually easily be inserted prior to the review lesson.

The student materials may be reproduced for use in the teacher's classroom without infringement of copyrights. No other portion of this unit may be reproduced without the written consent of Teacher's Pet Publications, Inc.

UNIT OBJECTIVES *Tangerine*

1. Through reading Edward Bloor's novel *Tangerine*, students will look at how people of different social classes behave, the struggle between man and nature, and the ability for those with disabilities to overcome challenges and find success.

2. Students will demonstrate their understanding of the text on four levels: factual, interpretive, critical, and personal.

3. Students will make connections with the material in the text and apply the lessons learned to their lives.

4. Students will be given the opportunity to practice reading aloud and silently to improve their skills in each area.

5. Students will answer questions to demonstrate their knowledge and understanding of the main events and characters as they relate to the author's theme development.

6. Students will enrich their vocabularies and improve their understanding of the novel through the vocabulary lessons prepared for use in conjunction with the novel.

7. The writing assignments in this unit are designed for several purposes:

    a. To check and increase students reading comprehension.

    b. To make students think about the ideas presented by the novel

    c. To encourage logical thinking

    d. To provide an opportunity to practice good grammar and improve students' use of the English language.

    e. To encourage students' creativity

8. Students will read aloud, report, and participate in large and small group discussions to improve their public speaking and personal interaction skills.

READING ASSIGNMENTS *Tangerine*

Date Assigned	Assignment	Completion Date
	Assignment 1 Beginning through Wednesday, August 23	
	Assignment 2 Monday, August 28 through Thursday, September 7	
	Assignment 3 Friday, September 8 through the end of Part 1	
	Assignment 4 Monday, September 18 through Friday, September 22, Later	
	Assignment 5 Saturday, September 23 through Thursday, October 5	
	Assignment 6 Thursday, November 2 through the end of Part 2	
	Assignment 7 Monday, November 20 through Thursday, November 23	
	Assignment 8 Friday, November 24 through Friday, December 1	
	Assignment 9 Saturday, December 2 through end of book	

UNIT OUTLINE *Tangerine*

1 Introduction Project Assignment PVR 1	2 Study ?s 1 Vocabulary 1 Active Reading Chart PVR 2	3 Mystery Group Writing Assignment	4 Study ?s 2 Vocabulary 2 Oral Reading Evaluation PVR 3	5 Study ?s 3 Vocabulary 3 Comic Strips PVR 4
6 Athletes with Disabilities	7 Writing Assignment #1	8 Study ?s 4 Vocabulary 4 Nonfiction Assignment PVR 5	9 Study ?s 5 Vocabulary 5 Grafting and Budding PVR 6	10 Study ?s 6 Vocabulary 6 Writing Assignment #2 PVR 7
11 Study ?s 7 Vocabulary 7 The Freeze PVR 8	12 Speaker	13 Study ?s 8 Vocabulary 8 Paul's Growth PVR 9	14 Study ?s 9 Vocabulary 9 Tangerine vs. Lake Windsor Downs	15 Writing Assignment #3
16 Extra Discussion Questions	17 Extra Discussion Questions Environmental Study Project Due	18 Vocabulary Review	19 Unit Review	20 Unit Test

Key: P = Preview Study Questions   V = Vocabulary Work   R = Read

STUDY GUIDE QUESTIONS

STUDY GUIDE QUESTIONS *Tangerine*

Assignment 1
Beginning through Wednesday, August 23
1. What city is the Fisher family leaving? Where are they moving instead?
2. What scene does Paul remember while he is waiting for his mother in the driveway of their old home?
3. What surprises Paul about the way Florida looks?
4. When Paul gets to his new town he sees tangerine trees burning. Why are they on fire?
5. Describe the muck fire burning behind Paul's home.
6. How does the football coach feel about Erik's joining the team?
7. How does Paul feel about getting special attention at school because of his visual handicap?
8. Paul is legally blind, yet he plays goalie in soccer. How does he do when he plays with the guys for the first time?

Assignment 2
Monday, August 28 through Thursday, September 7
1. What excuse has Paul always given people about why his vision is so poor?
2. Who is Kerri? How does Paul feel about her?
3. Why does Paul have a hard time believing the story his brother told him about how he damaged his vision?
4. Aside from playing football, what do Erik and Arthur do for fun?
5. What special equipment does Paul have for his eyes when he plays sports?
6. What is unique about Mr. Donnelly's house?
7. What is Lake Windsor Middle School's policy on how many kids can be on the soccer team?
8. What does it mean to "be on the bus" in regards to the soccer team?
9. How does Mike Costello die?
10. What does Joey Costello desperately try to do when he runs over to his brother's dead body?
11. How does Arthur benefit from Mike's death?
12. How does Paul say he would feel if his brother died?
13. What does Paul's mother want to change about football practice?

Assignment 3
Friday, September 8 through the end of Part 1
1. What nickname do the guys on the soccer team give Paul?
2. Why is Paul kicked off the soccer team?
3. What does Joey tell Paul about the reputation the kids on the Tangerine Middle School soccer team have?
4. Why does Paul get called to the principal's office with the other boys from the soccer team?

5. What do Paul and Joey do when they see the portables being swallowed up by the sinkhole?
6. How does Paul's dad get promoted?
7. What happens to the students in each grade level at Lake Windsor Middle School after the sinkhole disaster?
8. Why does Paul want to go to Tangerine Middle School so badly?

Assignment 4
<u>Monday, September 18 through Friday, September 22, Later</u>
1. How does Theresa Cruz help Paul?
2. What surprises both Paul and his mother about the Tangerine soccer team?
3. What does Ms. Bright, the soccer coach, say to Paul about being on the team?
4. Tangerine Middle School asked Paul's mom to bring over his file from Lake Windsor. How is it that Tangerine Middle School doesn't know about Paul's IEP?
5. What is Paul's new nickname at Tangerine Middle School?
6. A small fight breaks out at soccer practice between Victor and Tino. What is the fight about?
7. What happens between Erik, Arthur, and Joey while Paul and Joey are in the backyard comparing their new uniforms?
8. Why do the people at Lake Windsor Middle School bend the rules for Joey to let him transfer schools and play on a different soccer team?
9. How do the fans treat Paul's soccer team at their first away game?
10. Why does Paul start a fight at the first soccer game?
11. What does Victor say to Paul after the first game to let him know he is finally accepted and respected on the War Eagles team?

Assignment 5
<u>Saturday, September 23 through Thursday, October 5</u>
1. Why is the whole town laughing at Erik after the first football game?
2. What happens when Paul goes in for Victor in the team's first home game?
3. Why does Cara call Paul?
4. Why does Paul's mother call the *Tangerine Times*?
5. Paul remembers Joey's first day of school at Tangerine Middle. Joey decides not to use Theresa as a guide like Paul recommends. What insult does Joey use to describe Theresa?
6. What are a few of the unique qualities about the Golden Dawn tangerine?
7. Why does Tino get suspended?
8. In trying to get rid of the muck fires, what new problem did Paul's neighborhood create?
9. What is happening to the houses that are tented for termites?
10. What interesting file does Paul find on his dad's computer?
11. Why does Paul go over to Tino and Theresa's house?

12. In a flashback Paul has about his old home in Houston, he remembers how his parents discovered the problem with his peripheral vision. What experiment did they do to test his vision?

Assignment 6
Thursday, November 2 through the end of Part 2
1. When Paul visits the tangerine groves for the second time, what type of work does he do?
2. How did Luis hurt his leg?
3. Why did Luis have to play goalie in soccer?
4. Why do Paul and his family go to Mr. Donnelly's house?
5. What does Paul discover about his soccer coach's past?
6. In Paul's flashback he remembers being greeted by visitors who, when they got close to him, wondered why his eyes looked weird. Who were these visitors?
7. Why is the soccer game against Lake Windsor Middle School such a big deal?
8. How do the Tangerine players react when they drive through the neighborhood where Paul lives?
9. Who did Paul fill in for at the Lake Windsor game?
10. Paul's old coach tells his new coach that he isn't eligible to play due to his handicap and his address in the Lake Windsor district. How does Paul get to stay in the game?
11. What happens in the last play of the Lake Windsor soccer game?
12. Describe the bus ride back to Tangerine after the championship victory.

Assignment 7
Monday, November 20 through Thursday, November 23
1. Why do Theresa, Tino, and Henry come over to Paul's house?
2. Why does Erik punch Tino?
3. Who does Paul think witnessed Erik punching Tino?
4. Paul's mother gets locked out of the storage unit. Who has the spare key?
5. What does Paul see while hiding under the bleachers at football practice?
6. What do Paul's grandparents think of "the Erik Fisher Football Dream"?
7. Why are so many kids absent from school the first day it is cold?
8. What does Paul volunteer to do with Henry D.?
9. In what ways do Tino and his family protect the tangerine trees during the freeze?
10. What are the people in Lake Windsor Downs doing while the people of Tangerine are doing back-breaking work in the cold to save their trees?
11. Why do the Golden Dawn tangerines survive so easily?
12. When is Luis planning to get revenge on Erik and Arthur for hitting him with the blackjack?

Assignment 8
Friday, November 24 through Friday, December 1
1. Paul's dad admits that he knows all about Erik's football season but can't say what position Paul played in soccer. What reason does he give Paul for being so wrapped up in Erik's football and forgetting about Paul's playing soccer?
2. Lake Windsor Downs is vandalized after the big football game with Tangerine High. What damage is done?
3. The people of Tangerine rely on their plants to make money and live. In the freeze, many families are devastated by the damage done to their plants. Why are the people in Lake Windsor Downs happy about the freeze?
4. How many tented houses have been robbed of their valuables?
5. The neighborhood association thinks someone is stealing their expensive coy fish and selling them. What does Paul say is happening instead?
6. How does Luis die?
7. Why does Theresa call Paul?
8. What does Paul do during Luis's funeral?
9. What do Tino and Victor do at the awards ceremony?
10. What does Paul do to help Victor and Tino escape and avoid trouble?
11. What happens when Erik and Arthur pull up in the Land Cruiser while Paul is all alone in the dark on the perimeter road?
12. Paul remembers the true story of losing his eyesight. What really happened?
13. Paul confronts his parents about how he lost his eyesight. What excuse do they give him about not telling him the truth?

Assignment 9
Saturday, December 2 through end of book
1. Why doesn't Shandra put her picture in the newspaper when she makes the All-County Middle School Soccer Team?
2. Paul's soccer coach tells him he could have the goalie position next year. How does Paul respond?
3. Antoine goes to the Tangerine County Sports Commissioner and confesses that he has been lying about his address to play on the Lake Windsor football team. What action does the Commissioner's office take?
4. What strategy does Paul's dad want to use in fighting the football scandal?
5. How does Paul's mom find out that Erik was involved in breaking into the tented houses?
6. What agreement do the Fishers and the Bauers want their neighbors to agree to in regards to their stolen property?
7. The deputy arrests Arthur for being in connection with the murder of Luis Cruz. What does the deputy do to Erik?
8. What do Paul's grandparents say when they hear about all the trouble Erik is in?
9. How does Victor try to protect Paul from getting punished for jumping on the coach?
10. What is Paul's punishment for assaulting a teacher?
11. Why is Paul excited about going to St. Anthony's on a trial basis?
12. Why does Tino call Paul?
13. What does Paul write in his statement for the police?

STUDY GUIDE QUESTIONS ANSWER KEY *Tangerine*

Assignment 1
Beginning through Wednesday, August 23
1. What city is the Fisher family leaving? Where are they moving instead?
   The Fisher family is leaving Houston, Texas to live in Tangerine, Florida.
2. What scene does Paul remember while he is waiting for his mother in the driveway of their old home?
   Paul remembers riding his bike when a car full of shouting teenagers came up behind him. Someone was hanging out the window with a baseball bat and slammed it into a mailbox right next to Paul's head. He was terrified and thought his brother Erik was trying to kill him.
3. What surprises Paul about the way Florida looks?
   Paul pictured Florida covered in beaches and condos and is surprised to see fields of watermelons, tomatoes, and onions.
4. When Paul gets to his new town he sees tangerine trees burning. Why are they on fire?
   The land has been sold to developers, and they are burning the trees to clear the land.
5. Describe the muck fire burning behind Paul's home.
   The muck fire is an underground fire that is always burning. The land behind Paul's home is made of lignite, which is similar to coal, and the frequent lightning strikes keep the land burning underground.
6. How does the football coach feel about Erik's joining the team?
   The football coach is excited to have Erik on the team. He thinks he will be a star and help the team win.
7. How does Paul feel about getting special attention at school because of his visual handicap?
   Paul is angry at his mother for bringing it to the attention of the school. He hates that his mom fills out a special plan for him and feels like he can see just fine.
8. Paul is legally blind, yet he plays goalie in soccer. How does he do when he plays with the guys for the first time?
   Paul blocks every ball that comes at him and doesn't let anyone score a goal.

Assignment 2
Monday, August 28 through Thursday, September 7
1. What excuse has Paul always given people about why his vision is so poor?
   Paul tells people he looked at an eclipse and it damaged his vision.
2. Who is Kerri? How does Paul feel about her?
   Kerri is the girl assigned to walk Paul around school since he is visually impaired. He hates the idea and tells her he can see fine on his own.
3. Why does Paul have a hard time believing the story his brother told him about how he damaged his vision?
   Paul thinks that if the story is true, he should be able to remember it happening.
4. Aside from playing football, what do Erik and Arthur do for fun?
   Erik and Arthur spend a lot of time mud runnin' in Arthur's jacked up white Toyota Land Cruiser.
5. What special equipment does Paul have for his eyes when he plays sports?
   Paul has special goggles that are made out of unbreakable plastic.

6. What is unique about Mr. Donnelly's house?
   His house has been struck by lightning three times.

7. What is Lake Windsor Middle School's policy on how many kids can be on the soccer team?
   The school allows everyone who wants to be on the team to practice and get a uniform. No one gets cut from the team.

8. What does it mean to "be on the bus" in regards to the soccer team?
   Anyone who wants to play can be on the soccer team, but only fifteen kids can fit on the bus for away games. The best fifteen kids will be the players who get to go to the away games and play in all the soccer games. The others get a uniform but sit on the bench during home games.

9. How does Mike Costello die?
   While leaning on the goalpost at football practice, he is struck by lightning and is killed immediately.

10. What does Joey Costello desperately try to do when he runs over to his brother's dead body?
    Joey keeps trying to take off his brother's shoes.

11. How does Arthur benefit from Mike's death?
    Arthur is now the guy holding the ball for Erik's kicks. He took Mike's old job on the team and will be the one pictured in all the newspapers.

12. How does Paul say he would feel if his brother died?
    Paul says he would feel relieved if his brother died. However, he knows that Erik has something to do with the eclipse story and if he died, that part of the story and what he needs to remember would be gone.

13. What does Paul's mother want to change about football practice?
    Paul's mom wants football practice to be before school when there is no chance of a lightning storm.

Assignment 3
Friday, September 8 through the end of Part 1

1. What nickname do the guys on the soccer team give Paul?
   They all call him Mars because his goggles make him look like he's from outer space.

2. Why is Paul kicked off the soccer team?
   Since Paul's mother labeled him as handicapped with the school, he is not allowed to play on any sports team. The school's insurance company won't cover anyone who is already labeled as handicapped.

3. What does Joey tell Paul about the reputation the kids on the Tangerine Middle School soccer team have?
   Joey tells Paul that the kids on the Tangerine soccer team are in gangs and that most of them have guns. He warns Paul not to mess with any of those kids.

4. Why does Paul get called to the principal's office with the other boys from the soccer team?
   Someone vandalized the Wonders of the World exhibit at the carnival. The workers said it was soccer players, and the principal assumes it was them. As it turns out, the boys from the soccer team at Tangerine Middle School were the ones who did the damage.

5. What do Paul and Joey do when they see the portables being swallowed up by the sinkhole?
   The two boys run and help rescue kids who are trapped in the portables.

6. How does Paul's dad get promoted?
   After the sinkhole destroys the middle school, the local news does a report on why the civil engineering department didn't stop construction on a school over a sinkhole. As it turns out, Charley Burns was taking bribes and not doing any research on the land. When he is fired, Paul's dad gets promoted to the job.
7. What happens to the students in each grade level at Lake Windsor Middle School after the sinkhole disaster?
   The eighth graders will squeeze into rooms at the high school next door. The sixth and seventh graders will stay in the main building of the middle school since it wasn't damaged, but will be on a split schedule. Seventh graders have the option of transferring to Tangerine Middle School if they don't want to go to school in the evening.
8. Why does Paul want to go to Tangerine Middle School so badly?
   If he goes there, he can register without an IEP and will be eligible to play on the school soccer team.

Assignment 4
Monday, September 18 through Friday, September 22, Later

1. How does Theresa Cruz help Paul?
   She shows him around school and tells him about the soccer team and its players. Her twin brother is on the team and so are several of her friends, so she provides an "in" for him on the team.
2. What surprises both Paul and his mother about the Tangerine soccer team?
   The team is a mix of girls and boys. The girls on the team are starters and the best players in the county.
3. What does Ms. Bright, the soccer coach, say to Paul about being on the team?
   She tells him he can be on the team, but he can't take the place of one of her starting players. He has to play as backup.
4. Tangerine Middle School asked Paul's mom to bring over his file from Lake Windsor. How is it that Tangerine Middle School doesn't know about Paul's IEP?
   Paul's mom says that his IEP "disappeared" somewhere between the two schools. She actually opened the file and took it out so Paul could play soccer.
5. What is Paul's new nickname at Tangerine Middle School?
   The players on the soccer team start to call him Fisher Man.
6. A small fight breaks out at soccer practice between Victor and Tino. What is the fight about?
   Victor's goal is blocked by Paul, but as Paul is lying there with it in his hands, Victor kicks it out and into the goal. Tino says the save had already been made and the ball was dead, and Paul's save was good. The fight is over whether or not Paul made the save and has a lot to do with whether or not Paul is accepted as a good player on the team.
7. What happens between Erik, Arthur, and Joey while Paul and Joey are in the backyard comparing their new uniforms?
   Erik and Arthur come home and start making fun of Joey's dead brother, Mike. They make fun of his hair and start to make fun of Joey for trying to take off his shoes.
8. Why do the people at Lake Windsor Middle School bend the rules for Joey to let him transfer schools and play on a different soccer team?
   They know Joey's dad is a lawyer and they are afraid he might sue the school since his son was killed on their property.

9. How do the fans treat Paul's soccer team at their first away game?
   The fans yell mean things, spit on them, and throw acorns at them.
10. Why does Paul start a fight at the first soccer game?
    A player from the other team pulls Paul's goggles out and smears mud in his eyes. Paul punches him over and over for what he did.
11. What does Victor say to Paul after the first game to let him know he is finally accepted and respected on the War Eagles team?
    Victor tells Paul that he is a War Eagle and that the rest of the team will always back him up. He tells him that no one will mess with him at anyplace or anytime.

Assignment 5
Saturday, September 23 through Thursday, October 5

1. Why is the whole town laughing at Erik after the first football game?
   As Erik went to kick the football, Antoine pulled it away for a two-point conversion. Erik didn't know what was happening and kicked at nothing, causing him to fly up in the air and land on his back in the mud. The local news played the clip and made fun of him that night.
2. What happens when Paul goes in for Victor in the team's first home game?
   Paul scores the first goal of his life.
3. Why does Cara call Paul?
   Cara calls to tell him that Kerri said to tell him "hi." It is obvious that she is trying to see if Paul likes Kerri or not.
4. Why does Paul's mother call the *Tangerine Times*?
   She wants the newspaper to do a feature on the girl soccer players at Tangerine.
5. Paul remembers Joey's first day of school at Tangerine Middle. Joey decides not to use Theresa as a guide like Paul recommends. What insult does Joey use to describe Theresa?
   Joey calls Theresa a guide dog.
6. What are a few of the unique qualities about the Golden Dawn tangerine?
   It is seedless, very juicy, and can withstand cold weather.
7. Why does Tino get suspended?
   Joey insults Tino's brother, Luis, and the new fruit he has created. The two start to fight, and Tino gets suspended.
8. In trying to get rid of the muck fires, what new problem did Paul's neighborhood create?
   They dumped tons of water on the land to put out the muck fires, and now they have a mosquito problem along with the still-burning muck fires.
9. What is happening to the houses that are tented for termites?
   They are all being robbed.
10. What interesting file does Paul find on his dad's computer?
    Paul finds a file called "Erik's Scholarship Offers."
11. Why does Paul go over to Tino and Theresa's house?
    Paul goes to their house to meet Luis and learn more about tangerines for his project.
12. In a flashback Paul has about his old home in Houston, he remembers how his parents discovered the problem with his peripheral vision. What experiment did they do to test his vision?
    They created a fake clock and put Paul in the center. They then had Erik move from behind him in a circular motion asking Paul when he could see his brother.

Assignment 6
Thursday, November 2 through the end of Part 2

1. When Paul visits the tangerine groves for the second time, what type of work does he do?
   Paul crawls up and down rows of trees to help lay out hoses around the baby trees. He then cuts holes in the hose to help with watering the trees.

2. How did Luis hurt his leg?
   Luis was picking tangerines when he fell out of a tree. He landed on his kneecap and cracked it.

3. Why did Luis have to play goalie in soccer?
   Luis played goalie because he was handicapped. He couldn't move around the field, so he had to stay in the goal.

4. Why do Paul and his family go to Mr. Donnelly's house?
   Mr. Donnelly wants to introduce Erik to some people involved in the football program at the University of Florida.

5. What does Paul discover about his soccer coach's past?
   He finds out she was an Olympic track and field athlete.

6. In Paul's flashback he remembers being greeted by visitors who, when they got close to him, wondered why his eyes looked weird. Who were these visitors?
   Paul remembers when his grandparents came to visit and they commented on his eyes.

7. Why is the soccer game against Lake Windsor Middle School such a big deal?
   Both teams are undefeated, so the team that wins will be the county champion.

8. How do the Tangerine players react when they drive through the neighborhood where Paul lives?
   The players are all shocked at how large the houses are and how fancy the landscape is. They all comment that the neighborhood looks like it's out of a movie.

9. Who did Paul fill in for at the Lake Windsor game?
   He originally went in for Victor, but then took Shandra's spot as goalie.

10. Paul's old coach tells his new coach that he isn't eligible to play due to his handicap and his address in the Lake Windsor district. How does Paul get to stay in the game?
    Ms. Bright points out that the star football player at Lake Windsor High School, Antoine Thomas, lives in Tangerine. (She knows that since his sister plays on the soccer team for Tangerine.) She threatens to call the county commissioner and have the Lake Windsor football games forfeited due to Antoine Thomas's being ineligible to play. The Lake Windsor coach backs off (since he doesn't want the whole town to hate him) and allows Paul to play.

11. What happens in the last play of the Lake Windsor soccer game?
    Paul jumps the opposite way in the goal, missing where the ball is headed. Luckily, Gino is intimidated by Paul being in the goal and misses, tying the game. Since Lake Windsor has two ties and this is Tangerine's first, Tangerine wins the championship title.

12. Describe the bus ride back to Tangerine after the championship victory.
    Fans honk horns and flash their car lights. People come out of their shops to celebrate as the team bus drives back to the school. The kids on the bus all celebrate, and Paul is so happy to have been a part of the team he begins to cry.

Assignment 7
Monday, November 20 through Thursday, November 23

1. Why do Theresa, Tino, and Henry come over to Paul's house?
   They come over to use the computer to complete their science/language arts project.

2. Why does Erik punch Tino?
   Erik and Arthur make fun of Tino and the other kids for being farm-labor kids. Tino gets mad and makes fun of Erik and his humiliating play in football. Erik can't handle it and punches Tino, nearly knocking him out.

3. Who does Paul think witnessed Erik punching Tino?
   Paul thinks his dad was watching at the window the whole time.

4. Paul's mother gets locked out of the storage unit. Who has the spare key?
   Erik has the spare key; he keeps it in his locker at school.

5. What does Paul see while hiding under the bleachers at football practice?
   Paul sees Luis come to football practice looking for Erik. He confronts Erik about punching his brother. Arthur pulls a blackjack out of his bag and hits Luis in the head. He falls down and is hurt while Erik walks away laughing.

6. What do Paul's grandparents think of "the Erik Fisher Football Dream"?
   They couldn't care less about Erik's football career. They change the subject anytime it comes up.

7. Why are so many kids absent from school the first day it is cold?
   The kids are all helping their families fight the freeze to keep their produce alive.

8. What does Paul volunteer to do with Henry D.?
   Paul volunteers himself and Henry D. to help Tino's family battle the freeze.

9. In what ways do Tino and his family protect the tangerine trees during the freeze?
   They burn huge bonfires near the trees to keep them warm, try to keep soft ice on the trees so their temperature doesn't get below freezing, and cover the delicate parts of the tree with dirt.

10. What are the people in Lake Windsor Downs doing while the people of Tangerine are doing back-breaking work in the cold to save their trees?
    The people of Lake Windsor Downs are making hot chocolate, lighting their fireplaces, and preparing for the Christmas season.

11. Why do the Golden Dawn tangerines survive so easily?
    They are all little, and small trees are easy to save by covering them with dirt.

12. When is Luis planning to get revenge on Erik and Arthur for hitting him with the blackjack?
    All the football players have to return their equipment on Monday, and Luis plans to get revenge with Antoine and some other players then.

Assignment 8
Friday, November 24 through Friday, December 1

1. Paul's dad admits that he knows all about Erik's football season but can't say what position Paul played in soccer. What reason does he give Paul for being so wrapped up in Erik's football and forgetting about Paul's playing soccer?
   He tells Paul this is Erik's critical season since all the college recruiters are watching him.

2. Lake Windsor Downs is vandalized after the big football game with Tangerine High. What damage is done?
   Someone smashed several mailboxes and spray painted "Seagulls Suck" on the wall around the neighborhood.
3. The people of Tangerine rely on their plants to make money and live. In the freeze, many families are devastated by the damage done to their plants. Why are the people in Lake Windsor Downs happy about the freeze?
   The freeze kills the mosquitos and fixes the problems they were having.
4. How many tented houses have been robbed of their valuables?
   Twenty-five houses have been robbed while being treated for termites.
5. The neighborhood association thinks someone is stealing their expensive coy fish and selling them. What does Paul say is happening instead?
   Paul says he has seen Osprey flying to their nests with coy in their mouths.
6. How does Luis die?
   He suffered from an aneurysm after being hit in the head. A blood clot formed after he was hit by Arthur, and it took six days for it to kill him.
7. Why does Theresa call Paul?
   Theresa calls Paul to tell him not to come to Luis's funeral. She thinks something bad will happen if he comes.
8. What does Paul do during Luis's funeral?
   He pulls back a piece of sod and digs a hole. He puts his face near the hole and remembers Luis. He starts to cry while he thinks of Luis and then buries his tears in the hole.
9. What do Tino and Victor do at the awards ceremony?
   They run up to the stage in the middle of the presentation and severely beat up Erik and Arthur to get revenge for Luis's death.
10. What does Paul do to help Victor and Tino escape and avoid trouble?
    He jumps on the coach's back, forcing him to lose his grip on Tino. The coach starts fighting off Paul so that Tino can escape with Victor.
11. What happens when Erik and Arthur pull up in the Land Cruiser while Paul is all alone in the dark on the perimeter road?
    Erik and Arthur threaten Paul with a baseball bat and a blackjack. They tell Paul he's going to pay for Tino and Victor beating them up in front of everyone. Instead of being scared, Paul tells the two he isn't afraid and that he saw them kill Luis. Arthur gets scared and Erik goes crazy, swinging the baseball bat everywhere.
12. Paul remembers the true story of losing his eyesight. What really happened?
    Erik and his friend Vincent Castor got in trouble for spray painting on a wall around the neighborhood where Paul and his family used to live. They assumed Paul was the one who told on them so Erik pinned Paul's arms behind his back and held open his eyelids while Vincent sprayed white paint into Paul's eyes.
13. Paul confronts his parents about how he lost his eyesight. What excuse do they give him about not telling him the truth?
    Paul's parents tell him they didn't want him to hate his brother, and since the doctors said he might never remember what really happened, they decided not to tell him.

Assignment 9
Saturday, December 2 through end of book

1. Why doesn't Shandra put her picture in the newspaper when she makes the All-County Middle School Soccer Team?
   Shandra is afraid to put her photo in the newspaper with the other kids in case someone recognizes that she is Antoine's little sister and figures out Antoine is playing for the wrong team.

2. Paul's soccer coach tells him he could have the goalie position next year. How does Paul respond?
   He tells his coach he would rather have Maya's job and be out on the field.

3. Antoine goes to the Tangerine County Sports Commissioner and confesses that he has been lying about his address to play on the Lake Windsor football team. What action does the Commissioner's office take?
   The Commissioner's office nullifies the victories of every game Antoine ever played in since his first year on the team. Any records that anyone on the team set are also nullified.

4. What strategy does Paul's dad want to use in fighting the football scandal?
   He wants to lie and say he knew nothing about Antoine's living situation. He wants to put all the blame on Antoine and pretend no one else knew anything about what was really happening.

5. How does Paul's mom find out that Erik was involved in breaking into the tented houses?
   While she is at the storage unit she finds a gym bag that didn't belong there. She opens it and finds a gas mask, gloves, and several of the stolen items.

6. What agreement do the Fishers and the Bauers want their neighbors to agree to in regards to their stolen property?
   They want their neighbors to not press charges against Erik and Arthur. Both families promise to return all of the stolen items or pay for the replacement of the stolen items if everyone will agree to give Erik and Arthur a second chance.

7. The deputy arrests Arthur for being in connection with the murder of Luis Cruz. What does the deputy do to Erik?
   The deputy tells Paul's parents to keep Erik in the house and not let him go anywhere. He says he may stop by at any time and expects to see Erik there.

8. What do Paul's grandparents say when they hear about all the trouble Erik is in?
   They tell his parents that they should have sent Erik to a doctor when he first hurt Paul, all those years ago.

9. How does Victor try to protect Paul from getting punished for jumping on the coach?
   Victor tells the principal that Paul fainted and fell out of the bleachers and that he wasn't involved at all.

10. What is Paul's punishment for assaulting a teacher?
    He gets expelled from all Tangerine public schools.

11. Why is Paul excited about going to St. Anthony's on a trial basis?
    He knows he will have a bad reputation and kids will fear him. He has never been anything other than a nerd and is happy to be feared.

12. Why does Tino call Paul?
    Tino calls to tell Paul that he is welcome to come out to the groves anytime. In the phone call, Tino calls Paul "brother" letting him know everything is good in their friendship.

13. What does Paul write in his statement for the police?
    He writes about what happened the day Luis was hit with the blackjack. He also writes about Luis and what he meant to the people around him. He talks about why people depended on him and how they looked up to him.

MULTIPLE CHOICE STUDY/QUIZ QUESTIONS
Tangerine

Assignment 1
Beginning through Wednesday, August 23

1. What city is the Fisher family leaving? Where are they moving instead?
    A. They are leaving Houston, Texas to live in Tangerine, Florida.
    B. They are leaving Boston, Massachusetts to live in Tallahassee, Florida.
    C. They are leaving Houston, Texas to live in Tallahassee, Florida.
    D. They are leaving Boston, Massachusetts to live in Tangerine, Florida.

2. What scene does Paul remember while he is waiting for his mother in the driveway of their old home?
    A. Paul remembers playing goalie in a state soccer championship. When he makes the winning save, he realizes his parents are missing. He later finds out they left early to watch Erik's football practice. Paul feels angry and wishes his brother would get injured so he wouldn't be the star player.
    B. Paul remembers the last time his family moved. It was the middle of the night and his mother made it seem like a game to see who could pack and get out of the house the quickest. Paul thinks his family is hiding something from him and wonders why they had to leave so fast.
    C. Paul remembers riding his bike when a car full of shouting teenagers comes up behind him. Someone is hanging out the window with a baseball bat and slams it into a mailbox right next to Paul's head. He's terrified and thinks his brother Erik is trying to kill him.
    D. Paul remembers swimming in a pool with Erik and his older friends. They are playing "Marco Polo" and when Paul is "it" all the other boys quietly get out of the pool and dump baby snakes in with Paul. He's scared when he opens his eyes.

3. What surprises Paul about the way Florida looks?
    A. The fields full of watermelons, tomatoes, and onions
    B. The palm trees growing everywhere he looks
    C. The number of cattle farms along the road
    D. The beautiful coastline with white sandy beaches

4. When Paul gets to his new town he sees tangerine trees burning. Why are they on fire?
   A. They are covered in termites and have to be burned before the field is replanted.
   B. Someone threw a cigarette into the field and it caught fire.
   C. Lightning hit a tree during one of the daily storms.
   D. Developers bought the land, and they are trying to clear it.

5. Describe the muck fire burning behind Paul's home.
   A. It's a fire that burns on water. The lake behind Paul's home contains lignite, which is similar to gasoline, and the frequent lightning strikes keep the water burning.
   B. It's a fire that leaves behind a thick muck. The land behind Paul's home is made of lignite, which is a heavy clay, and the frequent lightning strikes ignite the clay and burn it until it leaves muck behind.
   C. It's an underground fire that is always burning. The land behind Paul's home is made of lignite, which is similar to coal, and the frequent lightning strikes keep the land burning underground.
   D. It's a fire that burns with a green color instead of orange. The land behind Paul's home is made of limestone, which has a green color, and the frequent lightning strikes keep the land burning in a bright shade of green.

6. How does the football coach feel about Erik's joining the team?
   A. The coach is thrilled because he knows Erik will be a star and help the team win.
   B. The coach is worried that no one will like him since he is new to the team.
   C. The coach is angry since Erik is taking the place of his son on the team.
   D. The coach is hesitant to let him join since he doesn't think Erik is any good.

7. How does Paul feel about getting special attention at school because of his visual handicap?
   A. Embarrassed and angry; he thinks he can see just fine
   B. Sad and depressed; it reminds him that he is handicapped
   C. Grateful and happy; he wants the help so he doesn't fall behind
   D. Nervous and worried; he hates being the center of attention

8. Paul is legally blind, yet he plays goalie in soccer. How does he do when he plays with the guys for the first time?
   A. He blocks some shots, but lets several in.
   B. He blocks every ball and doesn't let anyone score a goal.
   C. He runs into the goal post and has to leave early.
   D. He misses every ball, and the guys score easily.

Assignment 2
Monday, August 28 through Thursday, September 7

1. What excuse has Paul always given people about why his vision is so poor?
    A. He was born that way.
    B. He never ate any carrots.
    C. He was in a bad car accident.
    D. He looked at an eclipse for too long.

2. Who is Kerri? How does Paul feel about her?
    A. Kerri is the girl assigned to walk Paul around school since he is visually impaired. He hates the idea and tells her he can see fine on his own.
    B. Kerri is a girl in Paul's math class. He thinks she is really cute but is scared she won't like him because of his glasses.
    C. Kerri is the only girl on the soccer team. She is really good, and Paul thinks it's cool to have a girl on the team.
    D. Kerri is Erik's new girlfriend. Paul thinks she is just a stupid cheerleader like all the other girls Erik dates.

3. Why does Paul have a hard time believing the story his brother told him about how he damaged his vision?
    A. Paul finds a hidden newspaper clipping that makes it seem like something suspicious happened.
    B. Paul's parents laugh at him when he tells the story, making him think it is fake.
    C. Paul thinks that if the story is true, he should be able to remember it happening.
    D. Paul's brother is known as a big liar.

4. Aside from playing football, what do Erik and Arthur do for fun?
    A. They spend a lot of time mud runnin' in Arthur's jacked up white Toyota Land Cruiser.
    B. They spend time breaking into model homes and partying with other football players from the team.
    C. They play golf at the brand new course Arthur's dad owns and sneak beer from the country club afterwards.
    D. They travel to the Florida Gators' football field to work out with the college players.

5. What special equipment does Paul have for his eyes when he plays sports?
    A. Hard contacts he can place in his eyes for short periods of time
    B. Pitch black glasses that don't allow any sun into his eyes
    C. Special goggles that are made out of unbreakable plastic
    D. A bright blue helmet that protects his eyes and head from further damage

6. What is unique about Mr. Donnelly's house?
    A. It's on a sinkhole.
    B. It's been struck by lightning three times.
    C. It's the only one with red trim.
    D. It's the only one with tangerine trees.

7. What is Lake Windsor Middle School's policy on how many kids can be on the soccer team?
    A. Half of the number who try out make the team.
    B. Exactly 10 girls and 10 boys make the team.
    C. Everyone makes the team.
    D. Only the starting 15 make the team.

8. What does it mean to "be on the bus" in regards to the soccer team?
    A. Anyone can be on the team, but the bus only holds fifteen kids. Only the best fifteen players get to play in the away games.
    B. Kids whose parents do not have cars are allowed to ride the bus to away games.
    C. Anyone can be on the team, but the bus only holds fifteen kids. Only the players with clean uniforms are allowed on the bus.
    D. To "be on the bus" means you have the best grades in your class.

9. How does Mike Costello die?
    A. He is hit by lightning during football practice.
    B. He is killed instantly when a football hits him in the back of the head.
    C. He breaks his neck when tackled at football practice.
    D. He is hit by a big SUV while walking out to his car after football practice.

10. What does Joey Costello desperately try to do when he runs over to his brother's dead body?
    A. Hold his hand
    B. Give him CPR to bring him back to life
    C. Find his cell phone to call for help
    D. Take off his shoes

11. How does Arthur benefit from Mike's death?
    A. He is the new valedictorian.
    B. He is the new quarterback for the team.
    C. He is the one who gets to hold the ball for Erik's kicks.
    D. He is the new boyfriend of Mike's popular girlfriend.

12. How does Paul say he would feel if his brother died?
    A. Paul says he would feel excited if his brother died. However, he knows that Erik's death would really hurt his parents, and he doesn't want to see them get hurt.
    B. Paul says he would feel relieved if his brother died. However, he knows that Erik has something to do with the eclipse story, and if he died, that part of the story and what he needs to remember would be gone.
    C. Paul says he would feel devastated if his brother died. Even though they don't really get along, he can't imagine trying to comfort his parents and deal with the emptiness he would feel being the only child.
    D. Paul says he would feel happy if his brother died. His feels like his dad never pays attention to him or goes to his soccer games, so if Erik were gone, he would finally get the attention he wants from his dad.

13. What does Paul's mother want to change about football practice?
    A. She wants them to practice with pads on to reduce the number of injuries.
    B. She wants them to practice indoors so they don't get overheated in the Florida sun.
    C. She wants them to practice in the morning before school so there is no chance of lightning.
    D. She wants them to practice for one hour instead of two so the players can have more time to study.

Assignment 3
Friday, September 8 through the end of Part 1

1. What nickname do the guys on the soccer team give Paul?

    A. Mouse

    B. The Wall

    C. Mars

    D. Freak

2. Why is Paul kicked off the soccer team?

    A. He gets angry at another player for making fun of him and starts a fight. Both boys get kicked off the team for misconduct.

    B. He is labeled as handicapped because of his vision and therefore isn't covered by the school insurance.

    C. His grades are too low to be eligible to participate in after-school sports.

    D. He isn't as good as the eighth grade goalie, so they tell him he is cut from the team unless he wants to be the water boy.

3. What does Joey tell Paul about the reputation the kids on the Tangerine Middle School soccer team have?

    A. They are all in gangs and most carry guns.

    B. They are the best in the county and have already been scouted by colleges.

    C. They all take steroids to play better.

    D. They have so much money they get to travel together to see World Cup games.

4. Why does Paul get called to the principal's office with the other boys from the soccer team?

    A. They are all in trouble for vandalizing an exhibit at the carnival. It turns out the carnival employees confused them with the soccer players at Tangerine Middle School.

    B. They are meeting for a pep talk from the principal about the upcoming season. The principal has an old team list and accidently calls Paul out of class.

    C. They are having a meeting to discuss whether Paul should be allowed back on the team. Some of the guys got a petition going and now the principal has to decide what to do.

    D. There have been accusations that the coach is acting inappropriately at practice. Several of the boys are called in for interviews about the coach and his attitude.

5. What do Paul and Joey do when they see the portables being swallowed up by the sinkhole?
   A. Run with other kids to the high school for safety
   B. Videotape the scene to later be played on CNN
   C. Call 911 to get help
   D. Help rescue people trapped in the portables

6. How does Paul's dad get promoted?
   A. His boss dies, and he is next in line to take the position.
   B. His boss gets fired for taking bribes and never checking the land to make sure it was safe. Paul's dad gets promoted to his job.
   C. His boss quits after being harassed by the press and leaves the position to Paul's dad.
   D. His boss retires so he doesn't have to deal with the sinkhole disaster, and Paul's dad gets the job.

7. What happens to the students in each grade level at Lake Windsor Middle School after the sinkhole disaster?
   A. The eighth graders will squeeze into rooms at the high school next door. Sixth and seventh graders will stay in the main building of the middle school since it wasn't damaged, but will go on alternating days for eight hours instead of six. Everyone has the option of transferring to Tangerine Middle School if they don't want to go to school on alternating days.
   B. The eighth graders will squeeze into rooms at the high school next door. The sixth and seventh graders will stay in the main building of the middle school since it wasn't damaged, but will be on a split schedule (one in the morning and one at night). Seventh graders have the option of transferring to Tangerine Middle School if they don't want to go to school in the evening.
   C. The eighth graders will be given assignments from the internet. They will all meet at the high school to take tests but do most of the work from home. The seventh graders will transfer to Tangerine Middle School, and the sixth graders will get three months off but have to make it up in the summer when the repairs to the school are complete.
   D. The eighth graders will be relocated to the Lake Windsor community center, which is being converted into a small school. Seventh graders will all go to Tangerine Middle School, and sixth graders can stay in the main building of the school since it wasn't damaged.

8. Why does Paul want to go to Tangerine Middle School so badly?
    A. He wants the chance to start over and make new friends who don't know about his vision problem.
    B. He knows their soccer team is better and wants to be on a winning team.
    C. He can register without an IEP and be eligible to play on the soccer team.
    D. He wants to be as far away from his brother as possible.

Assignment 4
Monday, September 18 through Friday, September 22, Later

1. How does Theresa Cruz help Paul?
    A. She pairs up with him for a project in Language Arts. She is one of the top students in the class, so Paul is sure to start off with an "A" at his new school.
    B. She kisses him in front of a group of "cool" guys at lunch. Since she is in the popular crowd, the guys respect Paul for getting Theresa to kiss him.
    C. She stops three boys from beating him up in the hallway. She sees what is happening and runs to get her cousin to come break up the fight and stand up for Paul.
    D. She shows him around school and tells him about the soccer team and its players. Her twin brother is on the team as are several of her friends, so she provides an "in" for him on the team.

2. What surprises both Paul and his mother about the Tangerine soccer team?
    A. The team has a boy with an artificial arm on the team. Paul won't be the only player with a handicap.
    B. The team has a coach who knows nothing about soccer. She lets the team captain coach the team while she sits and reads a magazine.
    C. The team is a mix of girls and boys. The girls on the team are starters and the best players in the county.
    D. The team has a lot of rough kids. Paul has already seen three kids with guns on the soccer team and knows several more are in a gang.

3. What does Ms. Bright, the soccer coach, say to Paul about being on the team?
    A. She tells him he can't be on the team since they already have enough players.
    B. She tells him he can be the equipment manager until one of the starting players gets hurt. He most likely won't get to play much.
    C. She tells him he can be on the team but he can't take the place of one of her starting players. He has to play as backup.
    D. She tells him she's never seen such a great goalie. She promises him that he will start in the first game of the season.

4. Tangerine Middle School asked Paul's mom to bring over his file from Lake Windsor. How is it that Tangerine Middle School doesn't know about Paul's IEP?
    A. Tangerine Middle School doesn't have a special education program. They told Paul's mom if he stays at their school, he can't have an IEP. She agrees and they throw it out.
    B. Paul's mom says that his IEP "disappeared" somewhere between the two schools. She opened the file and took it out so Paul could play soccer.
    C. Lake Windsor Middle School is so busy with construction that they misplaced parts of his file. The IEP was part of the file that was lost in the construction chaos.
    D. Tangerine Middle School is so backed up with transfer students after the sinkhole that all they look for is the attendance and class schedule. They throw everything else away and start their own file.

5. What is Paul's new nickname at Tangerine Middle School?
    A. Geek
    B. Fisher Man
    C. Uncle Paulie
    D. Goggles

6. A small fight breaks out at soccer practice between Victor and Tino. What is the fight about?
    A. Whether Paul made the save or Victor made the goal
    B. Whether Victor is allowed to date Tino's sister, Theresa
    C. Who should be team captain
    D. Who should take Shandra's place as goalie

7. What happens between Erik, Arthur, and Joey while Paul and Joey are in the backyard comparing their new uniforms?
    A. Erik and Arthur come home and start making fun of Joey's dead brother, Mike. They make fun of his hair and start to make fun of Joey for trying to take off Mike's shoes.
    B. Erik and Arthur come home and push Joey on the ground. When he tries to get back up, they push him down again and make fun of how un-athletic he is.
    C. Erik and Arthur tell Joey that they are sorry his brother died. They ask him if he wants to go mud runnin' after football practice the next day.
    D. Erik and Arthur come home dressed in their football uniforms. Joey starts to cry because he starts thinking about his brother. The two boys try to make Joey feel better by telling him how much everyone misses his brother.

8. Why do the people at Lake Windsor Middle School bend the rules for Joey and let him transfer schools to play on a different soccer team?
   A. They know that he and Paul are close friends. They figure that Paul could use a friend at his new school since he has a handicap, so they let Joey transfer.
   B. They know he isn't that good at soccer and won't be a loss to their team. If he leaves, they could maybe win more games.
   C. They are thankful that Joey helped rescue kids from the sinking portable. They know those students would have died if he hadn't helped, so they do him a favor in return.
   D. They know Joey's dad is a lawyer, and they are afraid he might sue the school since his son was killed on their property.

9. How do the fans treat Paul's soccer team at their first away game?
   A. The fans take a lot of photos and encourage both teams to play their best.
   B. The fans have a table set up with water and snacks for both teams.
   C. The fans yell mean things, spit on them, and throw acorns at them.
   D. The fans pop the tires on the team bus and spray paint their mascot on the side line.

10. Why does Paul start a fight at the first soccer game?
    A. A player from the other team pulls Paul's goggles out and smears mud in his eyes. Paul punches him over and over for what he did.
    B. A player from the other team elbows Maya in the face, making her nose bleed. Paul has a crush on Maya and goes after the other player to defend Maya.
    C. The referee isn't making any calls against the other team. Paul gets fed up with the unfair game and starts yelling at the referee.
    D. Victor keeps yelling at Paul and telling him that he is causing the team to lose. Paul can't take it anymore and shoves Victor in the mud.

11. What does Victor say to Paul after the first game to let him know he is finally accepted and respected on the War Eagles team?
    A. Victor tells Paul to wear his jersey to school on game days like the rest of the team. He wants the whole school to recognize Paul as one of the players.
    B. Victor tells Paul that he is a War Eagle and that the rest of the team will always back him up. He tells him that no one will mess with him at anyplace or anytime.
    C. Victor tells Paul that he can play goalie in the second half of the next game. He has finally earned his spot in the position he likes.
    D. Victor tells Paul that he can come out with the team for pizza.

Assignment 5
Saturday, September 23 through Thursday, October 5

1. Why is the whole town laughing at Erik after the first football game?
    A. Erik starts to cry on the sidelines when he learns that Antoine will be holding the ball for his kicks. He has been practicing with Arthur and feels more confident with him holding the ball. Other players see him cry and spread the news around the school and town that Erik cried.
    B. Erik and Antoine are supposed to try a new play to win the game. Erik is usually only a place kicker so he gets confused about what to do. When Antoine gets him the ball, Erik panics and kicks it, but to the other team's end zone.
    C. Erik goes to kick the football and Antoine pulls it away for a two-point conversion. Erik doesn't know what is happening and kicks at nothing, causing him to fly up in the air and land on his back in the mud.
    D. Erik comes out on the field in his nice clean uniform but doesn't know he has a tear in his pants. As he goes to kick the football his pants split open and the whole crowd can see his underwear.

2. What happens when Paul goes in for Victor in the team's first home game?
    A. He gets knocked over by a bigger player.
    B. He scores the first goal of his life.
    C. He can't find his goggles and has to play blind.
    D. He misses a penalty kick that would have won the game for his team.

3. Why does Cara call Paul?
    A. To tell him that Kerri is dating Adam and to leave her alone
    B. To tell him that she likes him instead of Joey
    C. To ask him to help her break up with Joey
    D. To tell him that Kerri said, "Hi" and to find out if he likes Kerri

4. Why does Paul's mother call the *Tangerine Times*?
    A. She wants the newspaper to do a feature on the girl soccer players at Tangerine.
    B. She wants the newspaper to do a story about the kids of the tangerine workers.
    C. She wants the newspaper to do a story on all the kids that transferred to Tangerine.
    D. She wants the newspaper to investigate the poor conditions at Tangerine.

5. Paul remembers Joey's first day of school at Tangerine Middle. Joey decides not to use Theresa as a guide like Paul recommends. What insult does Joey use to describe Theresa?
    A. Joey calls Theresa a Mexican.
    B. Joey calls Theresa a fruit picker.
    C. Joey calls Theresa a guide dog.
    D. Joey calls Theresa a donkey.

6. What are a few of the unique qualities about the Golden Dawn tangerine?
    A. It is more colorful and doesn't need soil to grow.
    B. It is seedless, very juicy, and can withstand cold weather.
    C. It is bigger, sweeter, and grows in hot weather.
    D. It is healthier and produces three times the fruit as a normal tangerine.

7. Why does Tino get suspended?
    A. Tino gets angry at his Language Arts teacher for keeping him after class and causing him to miss soccer practice. He gets mad at her and curses, getting himself suspended.
    B. Tino and some friends skip school to go to the sports store to meet soccer players from the US National team. They get caught and suspended from school.
    C. Tino gets mad at Paul for liking his sister. He pushes Paul up against a wall and tells him to stay away from Theresa. A teacher sees this, and he gets suspended.
    D. Joey insults Tino's brother Luis and the new fruit he has created. The two start to fight, and Tino gets suspended.

8. In trying to get rid of the muck fires, what new problem did Paul's neighborhood create?
    A. Mosquitos
    B. Bugs
    C. Smoke
    D. Flooding

9. What is happening to the houses that are tented for termites?
    A. The paint is coming off.
    B. The walls are crumbling.
    C. They are being robbed.
    D. They are getting struck by lightning.

10. What interesting file does Paul find on his dad's computer?
    A. Court Dates--Erik
    B. Erik--Scholarship Offers
    C. Truth--Paul
    D. Paul--Vision Story

11. Why does Paul go over to Tino and Theresa's house?
    A. To work on his soccer skills with Tino and Victor
    B. To meet Luis and learn more about tangerines
    C. To eat dinner
    D. To hang out with Theresa

12. In a flashback Paul has about his old home in Houston, he remembers how his parents discovered the problem with his peripheral vision. What experiment did they do to test his vision?
    A. They put drops in his eyes to dilate his pupils. He then had to have air blown in his eyes and other tests to see what was wrong.
    B. They put Paul in a dark room. The held up a flashlight behind him and began to move around until he said he could see the light.
    C. They put a patch over one of Paul's eyes and made him try to dodge balls they threw at him. They threw balls from all angles to figure out where he couldn't see.
    D. They created a fake clock and put Paul in the center. They then had Erik move from behind him in a circular motion asking Paul when he could see his brother.

Assignment 6
Thursday, November 2 through the end of Part 2

1. When Paul visits the tangerine groves for the second time, what type of work does he do?

    A. He picks the ripe tangerines and loads them into crates to be shipped off for sale.

    B. He helps put shipping labels on packed boxes of tangerines and gets them loaded onto the truck.

    C. He crawls up and down rows of trees to lay out hoses. He then cuts holes in the hoses to help with watering the trees.

    D. He helps prepare the soil to plant tangerine trees in one field and then puts stakes for support on a field of baby trees.

2. How did Luis hurt his leg?

    A. He was shopping for groceries and got caught in a drive-by shooting. A bullet hit him in the knee and damaged it permanently.

    B. He was picking tangerines when he fell out of the tree. He landed on his knee and cracked his kneecap.

    C. He was playing in a championship soccer game and had another player slide into his knee with his cleats up.

    D. He was trying out for the Lake Windsor football team and was tackled in practice. His leg bent the wrong way and broke it in three places.

3. Why did Luis have to play goalie in soccer?

    A. He was handicapped and couldn't move around the field.

    B. He was the only one who had played goalie before.

    C. He got in too many fights when he was out on the field with other players.

    D. He had asthma and had trouble breathing if he ran too much.

4. Why do Paul and his family go to Mr. Donnelly's house?

    A. Mr. Donnelly has a meeting about the ugly lightning rods on the roof of his house.

    B. Mr. Donnelly wants to introduce Erik to some people involved in the University of Florida's football team.

    C. Mr. Donnelly holds a team meeting for the soccer players so he can interview them for an article about the championship game.

    D. Mr. Donnelly finally sold his house, and everyone was having a goodbye party.

5. What does Paul discover about his soccer coach's past?

    A. She was arrested for assault and battery.

    B. She was the principal at Lake Windsor Middle School.

    C. She was married to the Lake Windsor football coach.

    D. She ran track and field in the Olympics.

6. In Paul's flashback he remembers being greeted by visitors who, when they got close to him, wondered why his eyes looked weird. Who were these visitors?
   A. His grandparents
   B. Two of Erik's friends from football
   C. His aunt and uncle
   D. His piano teacher and another student

7. Why is the soccer game against Lake Windsor Middle School such a big deal?
   A. The winning team goes to the state competition at the University of Florida.
   B. The winning team gets a huge trophy to display in their school.
   C. The winning team will be the county champion since both teams are undefeated.
   D. The winning team wins a trip to Washington, DC to play in the national championship.

8. How do the Tangerine players react when they drive through the neighborhood where Paul lives?
   A. They are shocked at how big the houses are and say is looks like a movie.
   B. They ask Paul how it feels to live like a king.
   C. They make fun of all the matching houses.
   D. They talk about how small the yards are and how fake everything looks.

9. Who did Paul fill-in for at the Lake Windsor game?
   A. He originally played forward for Victor but then took over as goalie for Shandra.
   B. He originally played goalie for Shandra but then played outside midfield for Henry D.
   C. He originally played outside midfield for Maya but then played forward for Victor.
   D. He originally played defender for Tino but then played midfielder for Maya.

10. Paul's old coach tells his new coach that he isn't eligible to play due to his handicap and his address in the Lake Windsor district. How does Paul get to stay in the game?
    A. Ms. Bright threatens to turn in Antoine Thomas, the star Lake Windsor football player, for playing in the wrong district, so the other coach drops the issue.
    B. Paul's mom threatens to sue for discrimination against handicapped people. He gets scared and drops the issue.
    C. Paul's mom threatens to get him fired for holding practices in the lightning storms even after the death of Mike. The coach knows he would get fired and drops the issue.
    D. Ms. Bright threatens to tell everyone about Gino's steroid use and the coach drops the issue.

11. What happens in the last play of the Lake Windsor soccer game?
    A. Paul jumps the opposite way in the goal, missing where the ball is headed. Luckily, Gino is intimidated by Paul being in the goal and misses, tying the game and winning the championship title.
    B. Victor fakes a pass to Maya, who doesn't realize what is happening and misses. The ball goes straight to Paul, and he kicks the winning goal.
    C. Paul gets elbowed in the face by Gino. He gets to kick a penalty kick and makes the goal, tying the game, and winning the championship title.
    D. Maya passes the ball to Paul, and he does a header to make the winning goal.

12. Describe the bus ride back to Tangerine after the championship victory.
    A. The coach stops for pizza, and the players pig out--cheering and celebrating their victory. Tons of fans show up to cheer and throw confetti as the players get off the bus.
    B. The ride is almost silent since the players know this is their final game together. The fans all line the field, clapping and cheering, welcoming the players back home for the final time.
    C. Fans hold up signs congratulating the team along the streets of Tangerine. The players all are amazed at how much the victory means to their fans. They all stay quiet, smiling and taking in the whole scene.
    D. Fans honk horns and flash their car lights. People come out of their shops to celebrate as the team bus drives back to the school. The kids on the bus all celebrate, and Paul is so happy to have been a part of the team he begins to cry.

Assignment 7
Monday, November 20 through Thursday, November 23

1. Why do Theresa, Tino, and Henry come over to Paul's house?
    A. To use his computer to finish their science/language arts project
    B. To play a friendly game of soccer to stay in shape in the off season
    C. To hang out; Paul wanted a reason to spend more time with Theresa
    D. To hang out; Paul's mother wanted to meet his friends

2. Why does Erik punch Tino?
    A. Erik and Arthur insult Theresa. Tino gets mad and gets in Erik's face to defend his sister. He makes fun of Erik's humiliating play in football, and Erik can't handle it. He punches Tino and nearly knocks him out.
    B. Paul, Tino, Theresa, and Henry are kicking the soccer ball around in the backyard. As Erik and Arthur come in the gate, Tino kicks a hard ball that hits Erik in the head. Erik thinks it was on purpose, so he punches Tino to get revenge.
    C. Luis accidently hits Arthur's Land Cruiser with his truck when he pulls in the driveway to pick up Tino, Theresa, and Henry. There is no damage, but Arthur and Erik get mad. Tino gets in Erik's face telling him to calm down, and Erik punches him to show him who is boss.
    D. Erik and Arthur make fun of Tino and the other kids for being farm-labor kids. Tino gets mad and makes fun of Erik and his humiliating play in football. Erik can't handle it and punches Tino, nearly knocking him out.

3. Who does Paul think witnessed Erik punching Tino?
    A. His dad
    B. Joey
    C. Luis
    D. His mom

4. Paul's mother gets locked out of the storage unit. Who has the spare key?
    A. His dad
    B. Arthur
    C. Mr. Donnelly
    D. Erik

5. What does Paul see while hiding under the bleachers at football practice?
   A. Paul sees Luis come to football practice and talk to Antoine Thomas for a few minutes. The two, who both hate Erik, go up to him and threaten him. Erik shoves them away and Arthur pulls a gun out of his bag, warning them to stay away.
   B. Paul sees Luis come to football practice looking for Erik. He confronts Erik about punching his brother. Arthur pulls a blackjack out of his bag and hits Luis in the head. He falls down and is hurt while Erik walks away laughing.
   C. Paul sees Luis come to football practice and push Erik from behind. Luis tells him to never touch his brother again, and Erik stands there silently. As Luis walks away, both Arthur and Erik tackle him to the ground and kick him repeatedly.
   D. Paul sees Luis come to football practice and shove Erik in the chest for punching his brother. While Luis is talking to his friend, Antoine Thomas, Paul watches as Erik and Arthur break the windshield on Luis's truck and key the paint on the side.

6. What do Paul's grandparents think of "the Erik Fisher Football Dream"?
   A. They hate that Erik plays football. They feel like football isn't safe and constantly tell Erik he should quit.
   B. They are just as excited as Paul's parents. They are helping Erik get scholarships to good colleges and hope to see him play in the NFL.
   C. They couldn't care less about Erik's football career. They change the subject anytime it comes up.
   D. They are equally excited about Erik's football career as they are Paul's soccer career. They are supportive of both grandchildren equally.

7. Why are so many kids absent from school the first day it is cold?
   A. Most kids are helping their family fight the freeze to keep their fruit and vegetable plants alive.
   B. The kids rarely get a cold weather in Florida. When the first cold front comes many of them skip school to enjoy it.
   C. Most kids have to walk or bike to school. When it is very cold they stay home to avoid the harsh weather.
   D. The school doesn't have a heater since it is rarely cold in Florida. Most kids know this and stay home where it is warm.

8. What does Paul volunteer to do with Henry D.?
   A. Coach an elementary age soccer team
   B. Help Tino's family battle the freeze
   C. An extra credit project in science
   D. Work at a packaging plant over winter break

9. What ways do Tino and his family protect the tangerine trees during the freeze?
    A. They walk up and down the rows of trees with torches to keep them warm, put old tires around the base of the trees to keep the ice off, and keep them fertilized all night.
    B. They water the trees all night with a special mixture of water and anti-freeze, cover them with large blankets, and cut off parts of the tree that are already frozen and dead to keep it from taking over the tree.
    C. They burn huge bon fires near the trees to keep them warm, try to keep soft ice on the trees so their temperature doesn't get below freezing, and cover the delicate parts of the trees with dirt.
    D. They pick off all the fruit so it is not damaged, tie large blankets over the trees to cover them from the cold, and keep a fire burning to keep the temperature as high as possible.

10. What are the people in Lake Windsor Downs doing while the people of Tangerine are doing back-breaking work in the cold to save their trees?
    A. Playing in fake snow and drinking apple cider at the annual winter festival
    B. Watching the last football game of the season
    C. Making hot chocolate, lighting fireplaces, and decorating for Christmas
    D. The same as the people in Tangerine but with their own plants and landscaping

11. Why did the Golden Dawn tangerines survive so easily?
    A. They are all in portable pots and could be moved inside the house.
    B. They are all small and could be saved by covering them with dirt.
    C. They are all small and could be saved by covering them with blankets.
    D. They are designed to survive in heavy snow.

12. When is Luis planning to get revenge on Erik and Arthur for hitting him with the blackjack?
    A. When he is out mud runnin' on the weekend
    B. At the last football game of the season
    C. As soon as he is done fighting the freeze
    D. When the football players meet to turn in their equipment

Assignment 8
Friday, November 24 through Friday, December 1

1. Paul's dad admits that he knows all about Erik's football season but can't say what position Paul played in soccer. What reason does he give Paul for being so wrapped up in Erik's football and forgetting about Paul's playing soccer?

    A. Erik is more like his dad, while Paul is more like his mom.
    B. Erik is in high school and that's more important than middle school sports.
    C. Erik has college recruiters watching him.
    D. Erik is older and is used to getting more attention.

2. Lake Windsor Downs is vandalized after the big football game with Tangerine High. What damage is done?

    A. Someone egged several houses and toilet-papered the trees and bushes.
    B. Someone spray painted on the sides of houses and threw rocks at windows, shattering several.
    C. Someone smashed several mailboxes and spray painted "Seagulls Suck" on the wall around the neighborhood.
    D. Someone broke windows and slashed tires to cars parked in driveways overnight.

3. The people of Tangerine rely on their plants to make money and live. In the freeze, many families are devastated by the damage done to their plants. Why are the people in Lake Windsor Downs happy about the freeze?

    A. The freeze killed the mosquitos.
    B. The freeze stopped the muck fires.
    C. The freeze got rid of the unbearable Florida heat.
    D. The freeze brought the first snow.

4. How many tented houses have been robbed of their valuables?

    A. 6
    B. 123
    C. 63
    D. 25

5. The neighborhood association thinks someone is stealing their expensive coy fish and selling them. What does Paul say is happening instead?

    A. Little kids are fishing in the lake for fun and burying the fish they catch nearby.
    B. Alligators are feeding on the large coy to survive.
    C. Ospreys are catching the fish and taking them to their nests for food.
    D. They are dying from the runoff of mosquito spray into the lake.

6. How does Luis die?
   A. Erik and Arthur hear that Luis is going to take revenge on them. They take matters into their own hands and go to the tangerine grove to find Luis. They suffocate him and leave him for dead in the grove.
   B. He was hit by a frozen tree branch that fell out in the grove. It hit him on the head and knocked him unconscious. No one found him for several hours and by then he had died.
   C. He suffered from an aneurysm after being hit in the head. A blood clot formed after he was hit by Arthur, and it took six days for it to kill him.
   D. A blood clot forms in the same knee Luis fell on as a child. It prevents blood from flowing to his legs and he becomes paralyzed in the grove. They take him to the hospital, but there is nothing the doctors can do to help his blood flow and he dies.

7. Why does Theresa call Paul?
   A. To tell him not to come to Luis's funeral
   B. To remind him their science/language arts project is due the following week
   C. To ask him to help out in the groves again
   D. To give him information about when and where Luis's funeral will be held

8. What does Paul do during Luis's funeral?
   A. He digs a hole underneath the sod and puts his face near it. He remembers Luis and begins to cry. He then buries his tears in the hole.
   B. He stands just outside of the room where the services are being held. He peers through the door and listens but refuses to go inside near the body.
   C. He stays at home and finishes the report on the tangerine Luis developed. He adds more to the report in honor of Luis.
   D. He stands in the middle of the Golden Dawn tangerine grove all alone. He thinks about Luis and vows to tell the truth about what happened.

9. What do Tino and Victor do at the awards ceremony?
   A. They take the microphone away from Mr. Donnelly and tell everyone what really happened to Luis. They have the Sheriff's Department waiting nearby to arrest Erik and Arthur.
   B. They break in to Arthur's Land Cruiser and find evidence to prove Erik and Arthur were behind Luis's death.
   C. They run up to the stage in the middle of the presentation and severely beat up Erik and Arthur to get revenge for Luis's death.
   D. They hide fireworks underneath the bleachers where the football players are sitting. As the players are waiting to accept their awards, they light the fireworks.

10. What does Paul do to help Victor and Tino escape and avoid trouble?
    A. Paul pulls the fire alarm, causing the sprinklers to come on and surprise everyone, taking their attention away from Tino and Victor so they can escape.
    B. Paul fakes falling off the bleachers so that everyone runs to help him, allowing Tino and Victor time to escape.
    C. Paul jumps on the coach's back, forcing him to lose his grip on Tino and allowing Tino to escape with Victor.
    D. Paul takes the microphone and tells everyone what Arthur and Erik have been up to, allowing Victor and Tino time to escape.

11. What happens when Erik and Arthur pull up in the Land Cruiser while Paul is all alone in the dark on the perimeter road?
    A. Erik and Arthur start to make fun of Paul for looking so scared. Paul begs them not to hurt him and Arthur laughs. The two move around Paul in his blind spots so Paul can't see them. They make scary noises and threaten him. Paul passes out from being so overwhelmed with fear.
    B. Erik has Arthur hold Paul down as he stands over him with a baseball bat. They take off his glasses and shatter them with the bat and tell Paul he is next. Paul starts to cry, and his brother screams at him, telling him he cried like that years ago when he lost his eyesight.
    C. Erik and Arthur threaten Paul with a baseball bat and a blackjack. They tell Paul he's going to pay for Tino and Victor beating them up in front of everyone. Instead of being scared, Paul tells the two he isn't afraid and that he saw them kill Luis.
    D. Erik and Arthur pull up and get out of the truck with weapons. Paul starts to climb over the wall to escape, but Erik pulls him back down. Paul's parents hear him screaming from inside the house and come to see what is happening. They finally see the type of person Erik is and call the police.

12. Paul remembers the true story of losing his eyesight. What really happened?
    A. Erik and his friend Vincent Castor got in trouble for spray painting on a wall around the neighborhood where Paul and his family used to live. They assumed Paul was the one who told on them, so Erik pinned Paul's arms behind his back and held open his eyelids while Vincent sprayed white paint into Paul's eyes.
    B. Erik and his friend Vincent Castor got in trouble for setting a field on fire in the neighborhood where Paul and his family used to live. They assumed Paul was the one who told on them, so Erik takes a match and holds it near Paul. Vincent holds open Paul's eyelids while Erik touches the burning match to Paul's eyes.
    C. Erik and his friend Vincent Castor got in trouble for killing a cat in the neighborhood where Paul and his family used to live. They assumed Paul was the one who told on them, so they held him down and kicked him repeatedly in the face and head.
    D. Erik and his friend Vincent Castor got in trouble for breaking into a car in the neighborhood where Paul and his family used to live. They assumed Paul was the one who told on them, so they held him down and poured car oil into his eyes.

13. Paul confronts his parents about how he lost his eyesight. What excuse do they give him about not telling him the truth?
    A. They didn't want Erik to go to jail or be forced to see a psychologist.
    B. They didn't want Paul to tell people this horrible and embarrassing family secret.
    C. They didn't want Paul to hate his brother.
    D. They didn't want Paul to be afraid of his brother.

Assignment 9
Saturday, December 2 through end of book

1. Why doesn't Shandra put her picture in the newspaper when she makes the All-County Middle School Soccer Team?
    A. She witnessed a crime a few years earlier and tries to live her life on the secretive side.
    B. She is afraid someone might recognize that she is Antoine's little sister and be suspicious over why Antoine plays for Lake Windsor and she plays for Tangerine.
    C. She is caught in the middle of a custody battle and doesn't want her father to be able to locate her.
    D. She is embarrassed to be one of the only girls on the team.

2. Paul's soccer coach tells him he could have the goalie position next year. How does Paul respond?
    A. He shrugs, says it's a long way off, and says he'll see what happens next year.
    B. He says he wants Maya's job instead.
    C. He is excited to finally get to play the position he wants.
    D. He tells her that he won't be coming back to Tangerine next year.

3. Antoine goes to the Tangerine County Sports Commissioner and confesses that he has been lying about his address to play on the Lake Windsor football team. What action does the Commissioner's office take?
    A. They make the team forfeit their victories against Tangerine High School.
    B. They nullify every victory and every record set by anyone on the team while Antoine was playing.
    C. They notify the colleges Antoine is interested in and have them revoke their scholarship offers.
    D. They nullify all of Antoine's records, but allow the other players to keep their records.

4. What strategy does Paul's dad want to use in fighting the football scandal?
    A. He wants to contact all the colleges to formally announce that no one else on the team had anything to do with the scandal, so colleges will still recruit other players.
    B. He wants to have the newspaper recognize all the accomplishments of the other players to prove that Antoine wasn't the one creating all the team victories.
    C. He wants to sue Antoine and his family for lying and damaging the records and statistics of the other players.
    D. He wants to lie and say he knew nothing about Antoine's living situation so he can place all the blame on Antoine and pretend no one else knew anything about what was really happening.

5. How does Paul's mom find out that Erik was involved in breaking into the tented houses?
    A. She is cleaning Erik's room when she finds a gas mask under his bed. She is suspicious and begins to look for more evidence, finding a bag hidden in his closet containing a lot of the stolen items.
    B. She finds a gym bag in the storage unit that doesn't belong there. She opens it and finds a gas mask, gloves, and several of the stolen items.
    C. She sets up a video camera at a tented house to try to figure out what is happening. She watches the tape later and recognizes Arthur's Land Cruiser as well as Erik in a gas mask.
    D. She is driving past a tented house one night when she sees the Land Cruiser outside. She watches to see why Erik and Arthur are there and sees them come out with gas masks on and a bag full of stuff.

6. What agreement do the Fishers and the Bauers want their neighbors to agree to in regards to their stolen property?
    A. If they agree not to sue the families for the stolen property, the parents of each child will make sure the police prosecute Erik and Arthur to the fullest extent.
    B. If they agree not to press charges and give the boys a second chance, then the families will guarantee the return of all their items or pay for their replacement.
    C. If they press charges against the boys, they must sign an agreement to still let them both play football in college.
    D. If they only report half of their stolen items, making it a misdemeanor instead of a felony, then the parents will repay each person for all their stolen goods.

7. The deputy arrests Arthur in connection with the murder of Luis Cruz. What does the deputy do to Erik?
    A. Arrests him
    B. Puts on an electronic ankle bracelet to track him
    C. Gives him community service hours
    D. Tells him not to leave the house

8. What do Paul's grandparents say when they hear about all the trouble Erik is in?
    A. They are very upset and begin to cry. They blame themselves for not being more involved in his life.
    B. They tell his parents that they should have sent Erik to a doctor when he first hurt Paul, all those years ago.
    C. They tell his parents Erik was in trouble because he played football. They say the sport made him more aggressive, and they should have taught him to play something different.
    D. They are shocked and can't believe their grandson could do something like that. They demand to talk to him and get his side of the story.

9. How does Victor try to protect Paul from getting punished for jumping on the coach?
   A. He tells the principal that Paul was just trying to protect them and shouldn't be punished.
   B. He tells the principal that Paul fainted or something and fell out of the bleachers and that he wasn't involved at all.
   C. He tells the principal that Paul's glasses fell off and he couldn't see what he was doing. He says Paul probably thought he was pulling Victor off the coach.
   D. He tells the principal that Paul only helped them because he and Tino threatened to beat him up if he didn't help.

10. What is Paul's punishment for assaulting a teacher?
    A. He gets suspended for three weeks.
    B. He gets expelled from all Tangerine public schools.
    C. He gets suspended for three days.
    D. He gets sent back to Lake Windsor Middle School.

11. Why is Paul excited about going to St. Anthony's on a trial basis?
    A. The soccer team at St. Anthony's gets private lessons from professional players.
    B. Joey goes to school there, and he will get to spend more time with him.
    C. The school is close to Theresa's house, so he can walk to the groves after school.
    D. He has always been viewed as a nerd, but now he has a bad reputation and will be feared.

12. Why does Tino call Paul?
    A. Tino calls to tell Paul that he is welcome to come out to the groves anytime. In the phone call, Tino calls Paul "brother" letting him know everything is good in their friendship.
    B. Tino wants to tell Paul that Theresa really likes him. He thinks he's a good guy and wants to set him up with his sister.
    C. Tino wants to congratulate Paul on the good job he did on the project. He tells him their group got an "A" and that Luis would have been proud of the work he did.
    D. Tino wants to know what happened to Paul. He had a bunch of kids at school sign a petition trying to get him back at Tangerine.

13. What does Paul write in his statement for the police?
    A. He tells what happened but lies and says that it is more Erik's fault than Arthur's.
    B. He tells what happened and then offers ideas for ways Erik could be punished.
    C. He tells what happened and then talks about Luis's life and how he influenced others.
    D. He tells what happened and then describes other bad things Erik has done.

ANSWER KEY: STUDY QUESTIONS *Tangerine*

	1	2	3	4	5	6	7	8	9
1	A	D	C	D	C	C	A	C	B
2	C	A	B	C	B	B	D	C	B
3	A	C	A	C	D	A	A	A	B
4	D	A	A	B	A	B	D	D	D
5	C	C	D	B	C	D	B	C	B
6	A	B	B	A	B	A	C	C	B
7	A	C	B	A	D	C	A	A	D
8	B	A	C	D	A	A	B	A	B
9		A		C	C	A	C	C	B
10		D		A	B	A	C	C	B
11		C		B	B	A	B	C	D
12		B			D	D	D	A	A
13		C						C	C

VOCABULARY WORKSHEETS

VOCABULARY ASSIGNMENT 1 *Tangerine*

Part I: Using Prior Knowledge and Contextual Clues

Below are the sentences in which the vocabulary words appear in the text. Read the sentence. Use any clues you can find in the sentence combined with your prior knowledge, and write what you think the underlined words mean on the lines provided.

1. But I turned back around anyway, and I looked west down our street at the <u>receding</u> line of black mailboxes.

   _____

2. She stared at him in <u>disbelief</u> as he continued cheerfully, "Muck fires don't go out."

   _____

3. He was <u>relentlessly</u> cheerful, even in the face of Mom's rising anger.

   _____

4. A <u>vicious</u> thunderstorm hit in the late afternoon and knocked out our power for about ten seconds.

   _____

5. They both asked about his high school <u>exploits</u> back in Houston.

   _____

6. "Do I really have to provide you with an example of what <u>constitutes</u> an emergency?"

   _____

7. The players were doing <u>calisthenics</u> under a troubled-looking sky.

   _____

8. But I never really <u>cooperated</u>, and they soon dropped me from the routine.

   _____

9. Mom quickly grew <u>impatient</u> to get me to the car.

   _____

10. We sat in the beating rain noise for a few minutes, then it <u>abruptly</u> stopped, like some annoying little kid had stopped banging on a pan.

    _____

Tangerine Vocabulary Worksheet Assignment 1 Continued

Part II: Determining the Meaning -- Match the vocabulary words to their dictionary definitions.

____ 1. RECEDING   A. Outstanding events in which a person puts his/her strong points to the best advantage

____ 2. DISBELIEF   B. Wanting to hurry up; not wanting to wait for something to be done or to happen

____ 3. RELENTLESSLY   C. Becoming more distant

____ 4. VICIOUS   D. Makes the elements or parts of

____ 5. EXPLOITS   E. Exercises to develop muscles

____ 6. CONSTITUTES   F. Worked together willingly and agreeably

____ 7. CALISTHENICS   G. Steadily; in a way never giving up

____ 8. COOPERATED   H. Amazement or astonishment

____ 9. IMPATIENT   I. Ferocious; unpleasantly severe

____ 10. ABRUPTLY   J. Suddenly or unexpectedly

VOCABULARY ASSIGNMENT 2 *Tangerine*

Part I: Using Prior Knowledge and Contextual Clues

Below are the sentences in which the vocabulary words appear in the text. Read the sentence. Use any clues you can find in the sentence combined with your prior knowledge, and write what you think the underlined words mean on the lines provided.

1. I turned right at the end of Kensington Gardens Drive and walked parallel to the high gray wall.

   _____

2. The reason for the Coke-bottle glasses on my eyes was that I had stared at the sun, unprotected, during that eclipse.

   _____

3. I looked again at my schedule, feeling jittery.

   _____

4. When they can't do that, they run up and down the dirt road behind our wall, the perimeter road.

   _____

5. Because of this, Mom has taken to spotting irregularities whenever we drive into or out of the development.

   _____

6. Erik got out of the passenger side and walked up to Mom, slowly and solemnly.

   _____

7. "The whole left side of his hair was burned off. Singed right off, you know?"

   _____

8. Mom still did not seem to comprehend. She struggled for words.

   _____

9. We spent most of the time playing a pointless (and goal-less) scrimmage game--the sixth and seventh graders versus the eighth graders.

   _____

10. His while body was stiff, rigid, like he was dead.

    _____

Tangerine Vocabulary Worksheet Assignment 2 Continued

Part II: Determining the Meaning -- Match the vocabulary words to their dictionary definitions.

____ 1. PARALLEL   A. Things that are not within the usual rules or customs

____ 2. ECLIPSE   B. Practice session or informal game

____ 3. JITTERY   C. Burned slightly; scorched

____ 4. PERIMETER   D. Understand

____ 5. IRREGULARITIES   E. Border or boundary

____ 6. SOLEMNLY   F. Stiff; inflexible; hard

____ 7. SINGED   G. Extending in the same direction, equally distant at every point

____ 8. COMPREHEND   H. Extremely tense or nervous

____ 9. SCRIMMAGE   I. The disappearance of the whole or a part of the sun when the moon comes between it and earth, or of the moon when the earth's shadow falls upon it

____ 10. RIGID   J. Seriously; gravely; in a somber manner

VOCABULARY ASSIGNMENT 3 *Tangerine*

Part I: Using Prior Knowledge and Contextual Clues

Below are the sentences in which the vocabulary words appear in the text. Read the sentence. Use any clues you can find in the sentence combined with your prior knowledge, and write what you think the underlined words mean on the lines provided.

1. I am not going to dwell on this. I am just going to say it and get on with my life.

   _____

2. Joey didn't say anything else so Coach Walski intervened.

   _____

3. "It's not like we're testifying in court or filling out affidavits. Our names aren't on anything."

   _____

4. Then the walkways started to heave up and down, making terrible splintering noises.

   _____

5. The kids came diving out, jamming in the doorways, pushing into the backs of other kids, knocking each other flat on the disintegrating boardwalk.

   _____

6. A convoy of ambulances, police cars, and fire engines turned into the entranceway, their sirens wailing and their lights flashing.

   _____

7. Dad came home angry and agitated.

   _____

8. The main building of the middle school and all the buildings of the high school have been certified as "structurally safe" by a team of engineers hastily assembled by Old Charley Burns.

   _____

9. When she got to the Director of Civil Engineering and read out Dad's name, the crowd buzzed ominously.

   _____

10. I was elated, and I wasn't budging.

    _____

Tangerine Vocabulary Worksheet Assignment 3 Continued

Part II: Determining the Meaning -- Match the vocabulary words to their dictionary definitions.

____ 1. DWELL   A. In a threatening way

____ 2. INTERVENED   B. Quickly

____ 3. AFFIDAVITS   C. Very happy or proud; in high spirits

____ 4. HEAVE   D. Rise up or swell; bulge; lift

____ 5. DISINTEGRATING   E. Came between to mediate or help

____ 6. CONVOY   F. Breaking up; deteriorating; falling apart

____ 7. AGITATED   G. Focus one's attention on (usually a thought) for an extended time

____ 8. HASTILY   H. Written statements made under oath

____ 9. OMINOUSLY   I. Escort; an accompanying or protecting force; a group (as of vehicles) traveling together for convenience

____ 10. ELATED   J. Upset or disturbed

VOCABULARY ASSIGNMENT 4 *Tangerine*

Part I: Using Prior Knowledge and Contextual Clues

Below are the sentences in which the vocabulary words appear in the text. Read the sentence. Use any clues you can find in the sentence combined with your prior knowledge, and write what you think the underlined words mean on the lines provided.

1. One big guy took his forearm and swatted me out of the way, I like was some kind of gnat.

   _____

2. I have no problem with that, either, except that it has a disinfectant smell that kind of gags you.

   _____

3. "Inconsistent with the scheme of the other nests, but a nice touch."

   _____

4. The other guys took their cue from his and started laughing, too.

   _____

5. "It's the hair that fooled you. No family resemblance." Arthur picked up on the banter. "No. No resemblance. None at all."

   _____

6. "It's the hair that fooled you. No family resemblance." Arthur picked up on the banter. "No. No resemblance. None at all."

   _____

7. Erik and Arthur continued on through the patio doors, passing through them into Mom's world, changing their ghoulish routine about Mike Costello into one about the National Honor Society, or the student government, or some other bull for Mom's ears.

   _____

8. They turned to us and started jeering as we began our lap around the field.

   _____

9. It was only a matter of time until she found the range and scored, in spite of those menacing fullbacks.

   _____

10. We all ran back to our bus to escape from the pelting of the rain.

    _____

63

Tangerine Vocabulary Worksheet Assignment 4 Continued

Part II: Determining the Meaning -- Match the vocabulary words to their dictionary definitions.

____ 1.   GNAT   A.   Very small, biting fly

____ 2.   DISINFECTANT   B.   Mocking, taunting, or verbally abusing

____ 3.   INCONSISTENT   C.   Light, teasing, playful remarks

____ 4.   CUE   D.   Strangely cruel or monstrous

____ 5.   RESEMBLANCE   E.   Signal used to prompt an action

____ 6.   BANTER   F.   Not regular or predictable

____ 7.   GHOULISH   G.   Threatening or dangerous

____ 8.   JEERING   H.   Chemical agent used to destroy bacteria

____ 9.   MENACING   I.   Bombarding; striking rapidly and repeatedly

____ 10. PELTING   J.   Similarity of likeness with something else

VOCABULARY ASSIGNMENT 5 *Tangerine*

Part I: Using Prior Knowledge and Contextual Clues
Below are the sentences in which the vocabulary words appear in the text. Read the sentence. Use any clues you can find in the sentence combined with your prior knowledge, and write what you think the underlined words mean on the lines provided.

1. Dad continued talking in this manner throughout dinner, pounding home his theme to Erik--that Erik had contributed big-time to the victory, that Erik had actually made victory possible by being the decoy.

   _____

2. We started moving our hands in unison, up and down, changing the chant into the frenzied cry of "War! War! War!"

   _____

3. She sent one of the sixth graders in for Maya, who got a loud ovation from the fans.

   _____

4. Mom always seems eager to get on the phone with Grandmom and Grandpop. Dad and Erik certainly don't. They make themselves scarce.

   _____

5. "They gotta get fumigated," he said. "Fumigated for bugs. We've all got bugs."

   _____

6. "Luis thinks it could even return this area to its former prominence as the tangerine capital of the world."

   _____

7. "We rented pumps and spraying equipment and started saturating the area last month."

   _____

8. "And whether his attitude likes it or not, he's liable for that and for my missing property."

   _____

9. "But is it really worth your time and money to hire a lawyer and go to court just to take some guy's dilapidated pickup truck away?"

   _____

10. The homeowners just sat there glumly until Mr. Costello said, "OK. Somebody move to adjourn."

    _____

Tangerine Vocabulary Worksheet Assignment 5 Continued

Part II: Determining the Meaning -- Match the vocabulary words to their dictionary definitions.

____ 1. DECOY   A. The condition of being immediately noticeable or recognizable; being outstanding or well-known

____ 2. UNISON   B. Suspend (as a meeting) to or until another place and/or time

____ 3. OVATION   C. Enthusiastic, prolonged applause

____ 4. SCARCE   D. Something or someone used to lure or mislead another into a trap

____ 5. FUMIGATED   E. Ruined or decayed from age, wear, or neglect

____ 6. PROMINENCE   F. Subjected to smoke or fumes, usually to exterminate bugs

____ 7. SATURATING   G. Soaking thoroughly and completely

____ 8. LIABLE   H. Legally obligated or responsible

____ 9. DILAPIDATED   I. Corresponding exactly and occurring simultaneously

____ 10. ADJOURN   J. Uncommonly or infrequently found or seen

VOCABULARY ASSIGNMENT 6 *Tangerine*

Part I: Using Prior Knowledge and Contextual Clues
   Below are the sentences in which the vocabulary words appear in the text. Read the sentence. Use any clues you can find in the sentence combined with your prior knowledge, and write what you think the underlined words mean on the lines provided.

1. Tino was staring at him with <u>reverence</u>, with no trace of the hard-guy face he usually carries around.

   _____

2. "He became a genius at <u>horticulture</u>. There's nobody better in Florida."

   _____

3. I figured it was my chance to clear my <u>conscience</u> once and for all.

   _____

4. We dove through the door, nearly <u>capsizing</u> a glass trophy case in the foyer.

   _____

5. They hadn't won a game all year, and they had been recently <u>trounced</u> 8-0 by Lake Windsor Middle.

   _____

6. Everyone was quiet, <u>subdued,</u> as we rolled out of the parking lot.

   _____

7. "It came down to the last game last year, too. That's why they're our <u>archenemy</u> now."

   _____

8. "If you <u>retaliate</u>, you're playing their game. If you get focused on soccer, you're playing your game."

   _____

9. I shook my head <u>vehemently</u>. "You didn't choke, Gino. You missed. That's all."

   _____

Tangerine Vocabulary Worksheet Assignment 6 Continued

Part II: Determining the Meaning -- Match the vocabulary words to their dictionary definitions.

____ 1. REVERENCE   A. Chief or main enemy

____ 2. HORTICULTURE   B. Feeling or attitude of deep respect

____ 3. CONSCIENCE   C. Get revenge; pay back in kind for a wrong-doing

____ 4. CAPSIZING   D. Quiet; repressed; controlled

____ 5. TROUNCED   E. Beat severely

____ 6. SUBDUED   F. Turning or flipping over

____ 7. ARCHENEMY   G. The science or art of cultivating plants

____ 8. RETALIATE   H. One's own moral or ethical awareness of right and wrong

____ 9. VEHEMENTLY   I. Strongly; violently; with forceful expression of emotion or belief

VOCABULARY ASSIGNMENT 7 *Tangerine*

Part I: Using Prior Knowledge and Contextual Clues
Below are the sentences in which the vocabulary words appear in the text. Read the sentence. Use any clues you can find in the sentence combined with your prior knowledge, and write what you think the underlined words mean on the lines provided.

1. I watched that hand, <u>mesmerized</u>. I watched it move like a snake--a slow, casual snake hand--with a gold varsity ring on one finger.

   _____

2. Then Erik turned his full attention back to Tino, standing <u>insolently</u> before him.

   _____

3. Erik's face started to <u>contort</u>. The snake smile was gone now, replaced by something else.

   _____

4. I was on the <u>verge</u> of asking him, "Dad? Did you see Erik hit Tino in the face so hard that he nearly knocked him out?" But I didn't.

   _____

5. I sat there <u>agonizing</u> about it. Why couldn't I tell?

   _____

6. Luis Cruz got out and stared <u>intently</u> at the people who were leaving.

   _____

7. The trees were injured already; they're weak and <u>vulnerable</u>.

   _____

8. We walked toward the sound of a diesel pump until we came to a rickety <u>corrugated</u>-iron shed, kind of a lean-to that was open on one side.

   _____

9. One by one, I <u>pried</u> my black-gloved fingers back, trying to straighten out my warped hand.

   _____

10. I saw Tomas and his brother emerge from the black and <u>billowing</u> smoke, marching toward Tino.

    _____

Tangerine Vocabulary Worksheet Assignment 7 Continued

Part II: Determining the Meaning -- Match the vocabulary words to their dictionary definitions.

____ 1. MESMERIZED   A. Filled with distress, suffering, or torture; worrying in a distressed way

____ 2. INSOLENTLY   B. Capable of being wounded or hurt

____ 3. CONTORT   C. In a way that is boldly rude or disrespectful

____ 4. VERGE   D. Spellbound; enthralled; hypnotized

____ 5. AGONIZING   E. Moving (usually upward or outward) in a rolling, swelling motion

____ 6. INTENTLY   F. Twist into a strange shape or expression

____ 7. VULNERABLE   G. Separated or moved something with great difficulty

____ 8. CORRUGATED   H. Having folds, ridges, and grooves

____ 9. PRIED   I. On the edge; the point where an action is likely to begin

____ 10. BILLOWING   J. With great concentration or eager attention

VOCABULARY ASSIGNMENT 8 *Tangerine*

Part I: Using Prior Knowledge and Contextual Clues
   Below are the sentences in which the vocabulary words appear in the text. Read the sentence. Use any clues you can find in the sentence combined with your prior knowledge, and write what you think the underlined words mean on the lines provided.

1. Antoine Thomas throws for 3 TD's, runs for 2, in 30-0 <u>rout</u>.

   _____

2. Dad <u>brooded</u> about that. He finally said, "It's like Brain Baylor did it deliberately. Like he wanted to make Erik and Arthur look like fools."

   _____

3. That would sound a lot better than the truth--that their own teammates <u>despised</u> them so much that they helped a stranger beat them up.

   _____

4. "Wayne said it might have been an <u>aneurysm</u>, like a blood clot. He thinks Luis got hit on the head, it formed into a blood clot, and that killed him."

   _____

5. This cold of yours is really bad. It's really <u>persistent</u>.

   _____

6. He sat there staring at me, <u>astride</u> his red twenty-inch bike.

   _____

7. They were standing together on the sideline staring straight ahead, hard-eyed, totally focused, like the <u>wrath</u> of God.

   _____

8. Coach Warner himself grabbed Tino, who was still standing over Erik's <u>prostrate</u> body.

   _____

9. I <u>veered</u> off onto the perimeter road and stumbled along over the packed dirt until I found myself at the wall behind our house.

   _____

10. I understood that I was supposed to be terrified by this <u>spectacle</u>--these two demonic creatures on the dark, lonely road. But for once in my life, I wasn't.

    _____

Tangerine Vocabulary Worksheet Assignment 8 Continued

Part II: Determining the Meaning -- Match the vocabulary words to their dictionary definitions.

____ 1. ROUT   A. Refuses to give up or let go; long-lasting

____ 2. BROODED   B. A swell, almost like a bubble, in an artery resulting from the weakening of the blood vessel wall; if it bursts, it is usually fatal

____ 3. DESPISED   C. An overwhelming defeat

____ 4. ANEURYSM   D. Public performance or display

____ 5. PERSISTENT   E. One leg on either side of; straddling

____ 6. ASTRIDE   F. Turned or swerved off course

____ 7. WRATH   G. Disliked intensely; scorned; loathed

____ 8. PROSTRATE   H. Lying flat on the ground in humility or submission; helpless

____ 9. VEERED   I. Was in deep thought; focused attention on a subject persistently

____ 10. SPECTACLE   J. Strong, vindictive, or fierce anger

VOCABULARY ASSIGNMENT 9 *Tangerine*

Part I: Using Prior Knowledge and Contextual Clues

Below are the sentences in which the vocabulary words appear in the text. Read the sentence. Use any clues you can find in the sentence combined with your prior knowledge, and write what you think the underlined words mean on the lines provided.

1. I nodded with real <u>conviction</u> now. I said, "Yes! Yes!"

   _____

2. The Tangerine County Sports Commission, meeting in emergency session last night, voted to <u>nullify</u> all victories by the Lake Windsor High School football team over the last three seasons.

   _____

3. I had thought that maybe Lake Windsor would get fined. Or they would have to <u>forfeit</u> their last victory against Tangerine High.

   _____

4. He has allowed us, and by "us" I mean the Fishers and the Bauers, to approach all of you with a plan to make <u>restitution</u>.

   _____

5. "He has admitted his wrongdoing, he has said he is sorry, and he has made full <u>disclosure</u> of the facts."

   _____

6. What choice did they have? In the end the Blue Tent people accepted the plan, <u>reluctantly</u>.

   _____

7. "The school board has set down its policies in this booklet, and we are all <u>obliged</u> to follow them."

   _____

8. "Your violation is called a 'Level Four <u>Infraction</u>,' in this case, 'assaulting a teacher or other school board employee.'"

   _____

9. "Your mother has decided to <u>waive</u> your right to appeal. Basically, Paul, you did it, you got caught, and you got punished."

   _____

10. Then we went on an enormous shopping spree, <u>unprecedented</u> in my lifetime.

    _____

Tangerine Vocabulary Worksheet Assignment 9 Continued

Part II: Determining the Meaning -- Match the vocabulary words to their dictionary definitions.

____ 1. CONVICTION   A. Fixed or firm belief

____ 2. NULLIFY   B. Give up a right or claim voluntarily

____ 3. FORFEIT   C. Not willingly; with resistance or hesitation

____ 4. RESTITUTION   D. Making facts and details evident and clear

____ 5. DISCLOSURE   E. Required; bonded

____ 6. RELUCTANTLY   F. Violation; breach

____ 7. OBLIGED   G. Declare something void; invalidate

____ 8. INFRACTION   H. Surrender or give up as punishment for a crime, error, or offense

____ 9. WAIVE   I. Never before known, experienced, or done

____ 10. UNPRECEDENTED   J. Compensation for loss or damage

VOCABULARY ANSWER KEY - Tangerine

	1	2	3	4	5	6	7	8	9
1	C	G	G	A	D	B	D	C	A
2	H	I	E	H	I	G	C	I	G
3	G	H	H	F	C	H	F	G	H
4	I	E	D	E	J	F	I	B	J
5	A	A	F	J	F	E	A	A	D
6	D	J	I	C	A	D	J	E	C
7	E	C	J	D	G	A	B	J	E
8	F	D	B	B	H	C	H	H	F
9	B	B	A	G	E	I	G	F	B
10	J	F	C	I	B		E	D	I

DAILY LESSONS

LESSON ONE

Objectives
1. To introduce the *Tangerine* unit
2. To distribute books, study questions, and other related materials
3. To preview the vocabulary and study questions for Assignment 1
4. To begin the first reading assignment
5. To introduce the Environmental Study Project

Activity 1
Place the word "mystery" on the board. As a class, create a word web about mysteries.

Note: A word web can easily be created by placing the word "mystery" in the middle of the board and circling it. Next, have several lines coming out from around the circled word so that it looks like a sun. At the end of each line, write the ideas generated from the class discussion.

Activity 2
Once you have discussed mysteries, select a mystery puzzle to complete with your class. A few suggested web resources are listed below. Feel free to use these, or search for your own.

Note: The best way to complete this activity would be to hook your computer up to a projector and go online to complete an interactive mystery as a class. Variations include distributing a text based mystery or even playing the game "Clue." The point is to get your students thinking about the process of figuring out a mystery and looking for clues to understand the full story.

Suspicion of Murder: Interactive mystery game that prompts user to move about a mansion looking for clues to solve a murder. http://www.suspicion-of-murder.com/

Mystery Net: Site full of text based mysteries and interactive games varying in length and difficulty. http://www.mysterynet.com/

Mystery Links: Site of several links in helpful categories.
http://www.mostlylinksmysterysite.com/read.html

Transition: Tell your students they will be reading a book called *Tangerine*. Although the novel is not a mystery story in the traditional sense, there are several mysteries that are solved and questions that are answered with clues throughout the text.

Activity 3
Talk to students about the setting of the novel. Explain that Paul moves to Florida at the start of the book and has to get used to the new weather, the unexpected landscape, the historical significance of the city, the change in people, and several other daily challenges that come with living in a new place. Tell students that Paul is fascinated by his new surroundings and spends a lot of time examining his new environment and understanding how nature plays a part in his life. You should also explain that one of the themes of the novel revolves around nature and how it affects humans no matter how they try to change or avoid it. Inform students that they too will be examining their surroundings and putting their findings together in a project. Distribute the Environmental Study Project assignment page and discuss the directions in detail.

Activity 4
Distribute the materials students will use in this unit. Explain in detail how students are to use

these materials.

Study Guides Students should read the study guide questions for each reading assignment prior to beginning the reading assignment to get a feeling for what events and ideas are important in the section they are about to read. After reading the section, students will (as a class or individually) answer the questions to review the important events and ideas from that section of the book. Students should keep the study guides as study materials for the unit test. **Review the study questions for Assignment 1 while you're looking at the study guides.**

Vocabulary Prior to reading a reading assignment, students will do vocabulary work related to the section of the book they are about to read. Following the completion of the reading of the book, there will be a vocabulary review of all the words used in the vocabulary assignments. Students should keep their vocabulary work as study materials for the unit test. **Do Assignment 1 together orally to show students how to do the vocabulary worksheets.**

Reading Assignment Sheet You need to fill in the reading assignment sheet to let students know by when their reading has to be completed. You can either write the assignment sheet up on a side blackboard or bulletin board and leave it there for students to see each day, or you can make copies for each student to have. In either case, you should advise students to become very familiar with the reading assignments so they know what is expected of them.

Extra Activities Center The Unit Resource Materials portion of this LitPlan contains suggestions for an extra library of related books and articles in your classroom as well as crossword and word search puzzles. Make an extra activities center in your room where you will keep these materials for students to use. (Bring the books and articles in from the library and keep several copies of the puzzles on hand.) Explain to students that these materials are available for students to use when they finish reading assignments or other class work early.

Non-fiction Assignment Sheet Explain to students that they each are to read at least one non-fiction piece from the in-class library at some time during the unit. Students will fill out a Nonfiction Assignment Sheet after completing the reading to help you (the teacher) evaluate their reading experiences and to help the students think about and evaluate their own reading experiences.

Books Each school has its own rules and regulations regarding student use of school books. Advise students of the procedures that are normal for your school. Preview the book. Look at the covers, frontmatter, and index.

Activity 5
Tell students that they should read Assignment 1 prior to the next class period. Give them the remainder of this class (if time remains) to complete this assignment.

Environmental Study Project

When Paul first moves to Florida he is shocked to see it isn't all sandy beaches and palm trees. As he settles in to his new life he must adjust to the weather, natural disasters, and general change in interests and personalities of the people. While adjusting to these changes, Paul learns to appreciate the history, culture, wildlife, and essence of what makes up his new home town. Through these observations Paul also sees how nature plays a large role in the lives of those in his community. In this project you will be examining your surroundings and reporting what type of role they play in your community.

Project Specifics:
Find a way to *creatively* display the following required items:
- Map: You must include a detailed map of your community. This should include landmarks, cities, and geographical landscape features (lakes, rivers, mountains, forests, deserts, etc). You should also label places that are significant in your own life (your school, home, frequently visited places). Provide a map of your state as well to serve as a frame of reference for others when locating your community.
- Weather: Provide information about the weather in your community. This includes temperatures throughout the year, common rainfall/snowfall, and any dangerous or important weather conditions your area faces. Along with the statistical information, you will need to include a summary as to how the weather in your area affects the lives of residents. Think about the good and bad features with the weather of your community when writing this summary.
- Natural Disasters: Think about the natural disasters your community has encountered in the past and those that currently pose a threat to residents (things like sink holes, earthquakes, avalanches, etc). Provide factual information about the frequency of these events and the problems they cause for residents of your community. Include a brief writing explaining how residents have responded to these disasters in the past and how they prepare for future problems.
- History: Include information about the history of your community. Think about any historical prominence your community may have held and how that has affected the way your community has developed to what it is today. You may also want to include ways in which your community has changed over time.
- Residents: Provide information about the people in your community. What jobs do they hold? What types of housing do they live in? What sports are popular? Think about the things that make up the people of your community and include them in this section.
- Wildlife: Give details about the wildlife found in and around your community. What wildlife is found in your area? How does the wildlife help your community? How does the wildlife harm your community? You should also include information on the type of wildlife you find most fascinating.
- Culture: Include information about the cultures found in your community. What culture do you belong to? How do the various cultures interact?
- Stereotypes: Think about the stereotypes people have about your community. How do outsiders view your community? How are the stereotypes about your community true? How are they different?
- Overall reflection: Include a reflection about how all of the above items make up your community. Discuss the things you like and dislike. You will also want to comment on the role nature plays in the lives of people.

LESSON TWO

Objectives
1. To review main ideas, events, and vocabulary for Assignment 1
2. To help students identify common literary elements used throughout the novel
3. To bridge connections between the unit project and the novel
4. To preview the vocabulary and study questions for Assignment 2
5. To read Assignment 2

Activity 1
Give students a few minutes to formulate answers for the study guide questions for Assignment 1, and then discuss the answers to the questions in detail. Write the answers on the board or overhead transparency so students can have the correct answers for study purposes.

NOTE: It is a good practice in public speaking and leadership skills for individual students to take charge of leading the discussions of the study questions. Perhaps a different student could go to the front of the class and lead the discussion each day that the study questions are discussed in this unit. Of course, you should guide the discussion when appropriate and try to fill in any gaps students may leave. The study questions could really be handled in a number of different ways, including in small groups with group reports following. Occasionally you may want to use the multiple choice questions as quizzes to check students' reading comprehension. As a short review now and then, students could pair up for the first (or last, if you have time left at the end of a class period) few minutes of class to quiz each other from the study questions. Mix up the methods of reviewing the materials and checking comprehension throughout the unit so students don't get bored just answering the questions the same way each day. Variety in methods will also help address the different learning styles of your students.

From now on in this unit, the directions will simply say, "Have students answer the study questions for reading Assignment as previously directed." You will choose the method of preparation and discussion each day based on what best suits you and your class.

Activity 2
Review the vocabulary answers from the reading. Make sure students write down the correct answers for study purposes.

Activity 3
Write the definitions to flashback, foreshadowing, and suspense on the board. Explain how the author uses these elements in the novel to enhance the story for the reader and provide clues to figuring out the mystery. Give students the Active Reading Chart. For each category listed on the chart, work with your students to find examples from the novel after each reading section. You should also try to connect the Unit Environmental Project with the novel. Aside from the literary terms, work with your students to find examples of how Paul and his family interact with their new environment.

Activity 4
Review the study questions and vocabulary for Assignment 2 orally together in class. Tell students that they should read Assignment 2 prior to the next class period. Give them the remainder of this class (if time remains) to complete this assignment.

Tangerine Active Reading Chart

Directions: After each reading section find examples of suspense, foreshadowing, and flashbacks from the text and write them in the chart below. Some sections may have several examples for a specific category, while others may not have any. Be sure to include the page number with each example and be specific in your description of the event.

Suspense	Foreshadowing	Flashbacks	Interactions with the Florida Environment

LESSON THREE

Objectives
1. To help students understand the elements of a mystery
2. To exercise students' writing abilities

Activiity

Place the examples of mysterious first lines on the overhead. Read these lines to your students, pointing out that they each contain suspense, making the reader eager to continue the story. After reviewing the mysterious first lines written by professional authors, instruct students to take out a sheet of paper and write their own mysterious first line(s).

Once students have written a mysterious first line, have them pass their papers back to the student behind them (Note: You may decide to use some other type of passing method depending on the layout of your classroom). Have students then read the first line they were given and add a paragraph to the story. Encourage them to use this paragraph to develop the setting and characters of the story.

After students have written this paragraph, have them pass it to the student behind them. Give students a moment to read the story they were given and then have them add another paragraph. Instruct students to develop the plot of the story, continuing to use suspense.

After students have written this paragraph, again have students pass their papers to the person behind them. After students have had time to read the story given to them, instruct them to add another paragraph to the story, with a suspenseful cliffhanger.

After students have completed this paragraph, have students return their papers to the original author of the first line. Give students time to read the story they began and then add a concluding paragraph to their story.

When all stories have been completed, allow students the opportunity to share their stories with the class. As students are sharing, be sure to point out how suspense can really add to the story. Take this time to bridge connections with how suspense has been used in the novel and how it has affected your students so far.

Mysterious First Lines

"He should never have taken that shortcut."
(Michael Crichton, *Timeline*)

"I don't think my stepfather much minded dying. That he almost took me with him wasn't really his fault."
(Dick Francis, *To the Hilt*)

"The second time Ian Dunne came into my life, I was trapped under a pile of bodies, behind a sheet of plate glass."
(Lee Nichols, *Hand Me Down*)

"It was the third time in a month he had come to Los Angeles to observe her daily activities. 'I know your comings and goings,' he whispered as he waited in the pool house."
(Mary Higgins Clark, *Nighttime is My Time*)

"They murdered him."
(Robert Cormier, *The Chocolate War*)

"One by one my stepfather took the chicken bones out of the bag and laid them on the kitchen table. He laid them down real neat. In a row. Five of them. Two leg bones, two wing bones, one thigh bone. And bones is all they were. There wasn't a speck of meat on them."
(Jerry Spinelli, *Space Station Seventh Grade*)

"The house looked strange. It was completely empty now, and the door was flung wide open, like something wild had just escaped from it."
(Edward Bloor, *Tangerine)*

LESSON FOUR

<u>Objectives</u>
1. To review the main ideas, events, and vocabulary for Assignment 2
2. To preview the study questions and vocabulary for Assignment 3
3. To read Assignment 3
4. To evaluate students' oral reading

<u>Activity 1</u>
Have students answer the study guide questions for Assignment 2 as previously directed. Be sure to take a few moments to add to the Active Reading Chart. Next, preview the questions for Assignment 3 while you have the study guides out.

<u>Activity 2</u>
Review the vocabulary answers from the reading. Make sure students write down the correct answers.

<u>Activity 3</u>
Do the vocabulary worksheet for Assignment 3 together in class.

<u>Activity 4</u>
Have students read Assignment 3 of *Tangerine* out loud in class. You probably know the best way to get readers with your class; pick students at random, ask for volunteers, or use whatever method works best for your group. If you have not yet completed an oral reading evaluation for your students, this would be a good opportunity to do so. A form is included with this unit for your convenience.

ORAL READING EVALUATION *Tangerine*

Name _____ Class _____ Date _____

SKILL	EXCELLENT	GOOD	AVERAGE	FAIR	POOR
Fluency	5	4	3	2	1
Clarity	5	4	3	2	1
Audibility	5	4	3	2	1
Pronunciation	5	4	3	2	1
_____	5	4	3	2	1
_____	5	4	3	2	1

Total _____ Grade _____

Comments:

LESSON FIVE

Objectives
1. To review the main ideas, events, and vocabulary from Assignment 3
2. To provide students with a creative way to analyze a major event in the novel
3. To preview the study questions and vocabulary for Assignment 4
4. To read Assignment 4

Activity 1
Have students answer the study guide questions for reading Assignment 3 as previously directed. Be sure to take a few moments to add to the Active Reading Chart.

Activity 2
Review the vocabulary answers from the reading. Make sure students write down the correct answers.

Activity 3
Since many students may be unfamiliar with sinkholes, begin the lesson by showing students real photos of sinkholes. Next, have students open their books to the scene where Paul and his friends are leaving the office, immediately before the sinkhole opens under the middle school (Monday, September 11). Reread the entry with your students.

Next, hand out colored pencils and paper and have students rewrite this scene in a comic strip format. Remind students that they will need to depict all the action from the beginning of the sinkhole through the end of the entry. Tell students they will need to create several boxes to include all the action and use actual dialogue from the novel. Once students have completed their comic strips, allow them to share their work with the class.

As students are sharing, you may want to talk about Paul's role in rescuing others and how this event was a turning point in his new life in Florida. You may also want to talk about how this event, though generally considered bad, was a positive event in Paul's life.

You may also want to display the comic strips in your classroom.

Note: If your students are unfamiliar with this type of activity, you may want to provide examples of comic books and provide a quick review of how comic strips show action and use dialogue.

Activity 4
Review the study questions and vocabulary for Assignment 4 orally together in class. Tell students that they should read Assignment 4 prior to the next class period. Give them the remainder of this class (if time remains) to complete this assignment.

LESSON SIX

Objectives
1. To analyze how Paul's disability affects how others regard him
2. To analyze how Paul's disability affects his self perception
3. To educate students about athletes with disabilities

Activity 1
Paul's physical disability affects how others in the novel treat him. It also affects how he thinks about himself. Take a few minutes with your class to site examples from the novel where people treat Paul differently due to his physical disability. You may want to think about his mother, his father, his brother, his friends, school officials, and his coach. Next, work with your students to talk about how Paul overcomes being legally blind. Talk about how Paul views himself. Be sure to include both the positive ways he sees himself and the negative.

Activity 2
Transition your class discussion to Paul's playing soccer even though he is legally blind. Tell students that several real-life athletes with disabilities compete on the professional level. Tell students that there are also thousands of people with disabilities who participate in the Paralympics.

Next, get students into groups of three or four. Give each group information about an athlete who has a disability along with some markers and a blank sheet of paper. Have students read the information you give them and create a bio sheet for the athlete. Have them draw a picture of some sort and include information about the athlete's disability and their greatest accomplishments in the sport. After groups have finished creating their bio sheets, allow each group to present their athlete to the rest of the class. Once students have presented, conduct a brief class discussion summarizing what students learned that day about athletes with disabilities in professional sports.

Listed below are just a few athletes with disabilities competing in professional sports. Feel free to add others to this list and use them in your classroom as well. Information about these athletes can be found by typing in the name of the individual in a Yahoo or Google search.

Jim Kyte: First deaf hockey player in the NHL

Kenny Walker: Former defensive end for the Denver Broncos; deaf

Jim Abbott: Former pitcher for the Milwaukee Brewers; born without a right hand

Kelly Bruno: Ironman competitor and triathlete; amputated right leg below the knee

Marla Runyon: First legally blind track and field runner to participate in the Olympics

Trischa Zorn: Blind swimmer in the Paralympic games

LESSON SEVEN

<u>Objectives</u>
1. To practice persuasive writing
2. To evaluate students' writing skills
3. To further consider the idea of athletes with disabilities

<u>Activity</u>
Since students have learned about athletes with physical disabilities and have read about Paul playing soccer even though he is legally blind, they should now be ready to write a persuasive essay on the subject. This persuasive essay will require students to convince a coach to allow an athlete with a physical disability to participate in a sport. Distribute Writing Assignment #1 to your students and use the following rubric to provide feedback.

WRITING ASSIGNMENT #1 – *Tangerine*
Writing to Persuade

PROMPT
Paul's coach at Lake Windsor Middle School kicks him off the soccer team because of his physical disability. He argues that the insurance company won't cover Paul because of his IEP. Many other athletes are discriminated against due to their physical disability as well. Your assignment is to write a letter to persuade a coach to allow an athlete with a physical disability to play on the team or participate in the sport.

PREWRITING
Using your notes/information about athletes who compete in professional sports despite their physical disability, create a list of reasons why someone with a disability should still be allowed to participate in sports. Try to include facts and information about others who have overcome their disability to succeed in sports. You may want to use examples from the text as well.

DRAFTING
Write an introductory paragraph that addresses the coach debating whether or not to allow a player with a physical disability on the team. Be sure to include what sport the athlete is trying to play and a general statement about the disability of the person in question.

In the body paragraphs, continue to outline your reasons for allowing this athlete to play. Remember to use facts and examples about other athletes with physical disabilities who are participating in professional sports to support your view. Make each new reason or example a separate paragraph. In your conclusion paragraph, make your final plea for the athlete in question to play. Try to use a strong fact or example to leave the reader with a powerful ending.

PROMPT
When you finish the rough draft of your composition, ask a student who sits near you to read it. After reading your rough draft, he/she should tell you what he/she liked best about your work, which parts were difficult to understand, and ways in which your work could be improved. Reread your paper considering your critic's comments, and make the corrections you think are necessary. Ask your classmate what he/she thought of each of the characters/events you chose for your assignment.

PROOFREADING
Do a final proofreading of your paper double-checking your grammar, spelling, organization, and the clarity of your ideas.

WRITING EVALUATION FORM - *Tangerine*

Name _____ Date _____

Writing Assignment # _____   Grade _____

Circle One For Each Item:

Introduction:	excellent	good	fair	poor
Body Paragraphs:	excellent	good	fair	poor
Conclusion:	excellent	good	fair	poor
Grammar:	excellent	good	fair	poor
Spelling:	excellent	good	fair	poor
Punctuation:	excellent	good	fair	poor
Legibility:	excellent	good	fair	poor
Persuasiveness:	excellent	good	fair	poor
_____	excellent	good	fair	poor

Strengths:

Weaknesses:

Comments/Suggestions:

LESSON EIGHT

Objectives
1. To review the main ideas, events, and vocabulary for Assignment 4
2. To research and read non-fiction related to the book
3. To connect the book to real life
4. To broaden students' knowledge about topics related to the book
5. To preview the vocabulary and study questions for Assignment 5
6. To read Assignment 5

Activity 1
Have students answer the study guide questions for reading Assignment 4 as previously directed. Be sure to take a few moments to add to the Active Reading Chart.

Activity 2
Review the vocabulary answers from the reading. Make sure students write down the correct answers.

Activity 3
Take students to the library or media center. With students, brainstorm a list of non-fiction topics that could be related to *Tangerine*. A short list to get you started is included below.

The tangerine industry (or another type of produce applicable to your area)

People with physical disabilities in sports

Special sporting events for those with disabilities

Florida weather related issues (muck fires, lightning, sink holes, freezes, etc)

The creation of new species of plants, fruits, and vegetables

Competition between younger and older siblings

Younger siblings trying to live up to the success of older siblings

Information on parents who favor one child over the other

Aggressive behavior in young children

The role of sports in an individual's life

Wealth vs the working class

Forgetting/Remembering Traumatic Events

Eclipses

Visual Impairments/Blindness

Activity 4
Distribute the Non-fiction Assignment Sheet to students. Explain that students should choose a

non-fiction topic related to *Tangerine*. They should read a substantial article related to that topic and complete the Non-fiction Assignment Sheet for that article. Students may use magazines, newspapers, and the Internet as sources.

Activity 5
Bring the class back together and have each student tell what he/she read about.

Note: Compiling the Non-fiction Assignment Sheets into a booklet makes a nice follow-up activity and a handy reference for students.

Activity 6
Review the study questions and vocabulary for Assignment 5 orally together in class. Tell students that they should read Assignment 5 prior to the next class period. Give them the remainder of this class (if time remains) to complete this assignment.

NON-FICTION ASSIGNMENT SHEET
(To be completed after reading the required non-fiction article)

Name _____ Date _____

Title of Non-fiction Read _____

Written By _____ Publication Date _____

I. Factual Summary: Write a short summary of the piece you read.

II. Vocabulary
    1. With which vocabulary words in the piece did you encounter some degree of difficulty?

    2. How did you resolve your lack of understanding with these words?

III. Interpretation: What was the main point the author wanted you to get from reading his work?

IV. Criticism
    1. With which points of the piece did you agree or find easy to accept? Why?

    2. With which points of the piece did you disagree or find difficult to believe? Why?

V. Personal Response: What do you think about this piece? OR How does this piece influence your ideas?

LESSON NINE

Objectives
1. To review the main ideas, events, and vocabulary for Assignment 5
2. To help students understand grafting and budding
3. To preview the vocabulary and study questions for Assignment 6
4. To Read Assignment 6

Activity 1
Have students answer the study guide questions for reading Assignment 5 as previously directed. Be sure to take a few moments to add to the Active Reading Chart.

Activity 2
Review the vocabulary answers from the reading. Make sure students write down the correct answers.

Activity 3
Paul is fascinated by what he learns from Luis about the tangerine industry. He is especially impressed that Luis created a new variety of tangerines, the Golden Dawn. Since this portion of the text uses a lot of scientific terminology and can be difficult for students to understand, take some time to talk to students about how new varieties of plants are created. Talk about why Luis wanted to create a new variety of tangerine and the benefits of developing new varieties. You may also want to review grafting and budding of citrus fruits since Luis goes into detail about the process in the Thursday, October 5, entry.

Listed below are some helpful articles and videos about grafting and budding. Feel free to use these or find additional information of your own.

http://aggie-horticulture.tamu.edu/citrus/budding/budding.htm

http://www.treehelp.com/trees/citrus/propagation-by-grafting.asp

http://concise.britannica.com/ebc/art-83887/Advantages-of-budding-and-grafting

Activity 4
Review the study questions and vocabulary for Assignment 6 orally together in class. Tell students that they should read Assignment 6 prior to the next class period. Give them the remainder of this class (if time remains) to complete this assignment.

LESSON TEN

Objectives
1. To review the main ideas, events, and vocabulary for Assignment 6
2. To practice creative writing
3. To practice writing a report
4. To practice logical thinking
5. To evaluate students' writing skills
6. To solve a mystery
7. To preview the vocabulary and study questions for Assignment 7
8. To read Assignment 7

Activity 1
Have students answer the study guide questions for reading Assignment 6 as previously directed. Be sure to take a few moments to add to the Active Reading Chart.

Activity 2
Review the vocabulary answers from the reading. Make sure students write down the correct answers.

Activity 3
Prior to this assignment create an evidence bag for each student in your class. You can do this by taking several paper lunch sacks and placing four to six random items from around your house in each bag (ketchup packets, movie ticket stubs, fake flowers, small dog toys, shoelaces... the more random and insignificant the better).

Give each student an evidence bag along with a Crime Scene Investigation Report. Tell students that the contents of their bag were found at a murder site and that they must figure out who the victim was, how he or she was murdered, and who the prime suspect is. Students will have to find a way to explain how each item in the evidence bag was used in the murder. Instruct students to use their imagination, telling them that there is no right or wrong answer. Have students use the Crime Scene Investigation Report as a prewriting activity. Afterwards, distribute Writing Assignment 2 so students can complete the actual writing assignment (an official police report to turn in to you regarding their findings).

Activity 4
Review the study questions and vocabulary for Assignment 7 orally together in class. Tell students that they should read Assignment 7 prior to the next class period. Give them the remainder of this class (if time remains) to complete this assignment.

Crime Scene Investigation Report

POLICE LINE DO NOT CROSS POLICE LINE DO NOT CROSS POLICE LINE DO NOT CROSS

Name of Investigator:_____

Evidence found at the crime scene (list all):
_____
_____
_____

Name and information about the victim:
_____
_____
_____

Where the victim's body was found and how:
_____
_____
_____

Importance of each piece of evidence (list each piece and tell why it was at the crime scene and if it belonged to the victim or suspect):
_____
_____
_____
_____
_____
_____
_____
_____
_____
_____
_____

How the victim was murdered:
_____
_____
_____

Name and motive for prime suspect:
_____
_____
_____

WRITING ASSIGNMENT #2 - *Tangerine*
Writing to Express Personal Opinions
Creative Writing

PROMPT
Tangerine is a novel full of mysteries, leaving both the reader and Paul searching for answers. In this writing assignment, you will tackle a murder mystery and create your own answers to the mystery at hand. Your task is to take on the role of a crime scene investigator. You will be given an evidence bag containing items found at the scene of the murder. Using your Crime Scene Investigation Report, begin to piece to together the mysterious murder that took place. There are no right or wrong answers to this mystery. Use your imagination to fill in the holes of this murder. The only requirement is that you use the items in your evidence bag as your guide to explaining the mystery. After completing the Crime Scene Investigation Report, you will then write up your findings in an Official Report. Be sure to include who the victim was, how he or she was murdered, and who the prime suspect is. You must also explain the significance or role of each piece of evidence found at the crime scene.

PREWRITING
Use the Crime Scene Investigation Report as a prewriting guide. On this sheet you will create answers to help you solve the mystery. Remember, there are no right or wrong answers. You will have to make up a lot of the information in this mystery. Your only requirement is that you explain the significance of each item found at the crime scene.

DRAFTING
Once you have completed the Crime Scene Investigation Report, you may begin writing the Official Report detailing your findings. This is the actual writing assignment that will be graded for overall writing ability. When writing your Official Report, be sure to include all the details you wrote on the Crime Scene Investigation Report. Remember, your Official Report should be in paragraph form and contain all of the information from the Crime Scene Investigation Report to explain how you solved the mystery.

PROMPT
When you finish the rough draft of your composition, ask a student who sits near you to read it. After reading your rough draft, he/she should tell you what he/she liked best about your work, which parts were difficult to understand, and ways in which your work could be improved. Reread your paper considering your critic's comments, and make the corrections you think are necessary. Ask your classmate what he/she thought of each of the characters/events you chose for your assignment.

PROOFREADING
Do a final proofreading of your paper double-checking your grammar, spelling, organization, and the clarity of your ideas.

LESSON ELEVEN

Objectives
1. To review the main ideas, events, and vocabulary from Assignment 7
2. To help students understand the roles of each individual during the freeze
3. To preview the vocabulary and study questions for Assignment 8
4. To read Assignment 8

Activity 1
Have students answer the study guide questions for reading Assignment 7 as previously directed. Be sure to take a few moments to add to the Active Reading Chart.

Activity 2
Review the vocabulary answers from the reading. Make sure students write down the correct answers.

Activity 3
Have your students reread "Thursday, November 23, Thanksgiving." As they are reading, ask them to write down all the jobs people did that night. Come together as a class and create a list of all the different jobs individuals were busy doing to save the tangerine trees. After compiling this list, talk about why each job was important and how several trees were saved from the teamwork that took place that night. You may also want to talk to your students about Paul's role during the freeze. Remind students that Paul volunteered to help work in the groves during the freeze, despite the tough conditions. Ask students to then think about what the people of Lake Windsor Downs were doing during the freeze. Compare and contrast how both sets of people (those in Tangerine and those in Lake Windsor Downs) viewed the freeze.

Activity 4
Review the study questions and vocabulary for Assignment 8 orally together in class. Tell students that they should read Assignment 8 prior to the next class period. Give them the remainder of this class (if time remains) to complete this assignment.

LESSON TWELVE

Objectives
1. To bring ideas from the book into real life
2. To explore in more depth one idea from the book
3. To practice listening skills

Activity

This day is set aside for a guest speaker. Invite one or more of the following people from your community to speak to your class:

An athlete with a physical disabilit

Someone from the citrus industry

Someone who could speak on Florida's environment and natural disasters

An individual who has overcome a traumatic event

An athlete to talk about the role sports can have in a person's life

Psychologist to talk about the effects of a traumatic event on an individual

Psychologist to talk about children growing up in the shadow of an older sibling

Divide your class time according to how many speakers you're able to acquire. Remember to allow time for students to ask questions. Let each speaker know how much time he/she will have for the presentation. Allow for time at the end of the class for students to make connections with what they have learned from the speakers with what they have read in *Tangerine*.

Follow Up: Be sure you and your students write thank you notes to each of your guests. At the very least, get a thank you card for each guest and have each of your students sign it (with any personal responses, if there is room).

LESSON THIRTEEN

Objectives
1. To review the main ideas, events, and vocabulary of Assignment 8
2. To examine Paul's growth
3. To preview the vocabulary and study questions for Assignment 9
4. To read Assignment 9

Activity 1
Have students answer the study guide questions for reading Assignment 8 as previously directed. Be sure to take a few moments to add to the Active Reading Chart.

Activity 2
Review the vocabulary answers from the reading. Make sure students write down the correct answers.

Activity 3
In this portion of the reading Paul discovers that the person he looked up to, Luis, is dead. Talk with your students about why Paul looked up to Luis so much. You may want to mention Luis's disability and participation in sports along with the way he stood up to Erik. Talk to your students about how Paul receives closure from Luis's death since he was asked not to attend the funeral. Have students reread the scene where Paul walks into his backyard in his suit and remembers Luis in his own way. Ask students to think about how Paul changes and grows in that moment.

Create a chart on the board with two columns. Label one column "before Luis dies" and the other "after Luis dies." In the first column create a list of personality traits Paul had before Luis died. You might want to pay close attention to the way he regarded his brother and his own disability. In the other column think of ways that Paul changed after Luis died. Make sure to review his actions at the awards ceremony and what these revealed about his personality.

After creating this chart, talk again about how Paul changed as a result of Luis's death. Talk about how that experience sparked a significant change in Paul, helping him grow as an individual. Next, examine the scene at the end of the reading assignment where Paul stands up to Erik and Arthur and finds he is no longer afraid. Ask students to think about how this change in Paul's character helped him remember what really happened to him as a child.

Activity 4
Review the study questions and vocabulary for Assignment 9 orally together in class. Tell students that they should read Assignment 9 prior to the next class period. Give them the remainder of this class (if time remains) to complete this assignment.

LESSON FOURTEEN

<u>Objectives</u>
1. To review the main ideas, events, and vocabulary for Assignment 9
2. To compare and contrast the lives of the people in Tangerine with those in Lake Windsor Downs
3. To practice critical thinking and analyzing

<u>Activity 1</u>
Have students answer the study guide questions for reading Assignment 9 as previously directed. Be sure to take a few moments to add to the Active Reading Chart.

<u>Activity 2</u>
Review the vocabulary answers from the reading. Make sure students write down the correct answers.

<u>Activity 3</u>
Throughout the novel the author shows the contrast between the people of Tangerine and the people of Lake Windsor Downs. Have your students work in groups of three or four to compare and contrast these two groups of people. Give them a Venn Diagram and ask them to think of both the similarities and the differences of these two groups of people. Prompt them to think about things like profession, housing, schools, opportunities, etc.

After students have had the chance to work in small groups, bring the class together to discuss how the author shows the contrast between the two classes of people in the novel. Once you have discussed the different social classes of people, ask students to think about which group is happier. Though some might feel like the wealthier class in Lake Windsor Downs should be happier, prompt them to think about the relationships and support that exists with those in Tangerine versus those in Lake Windsor Downs.

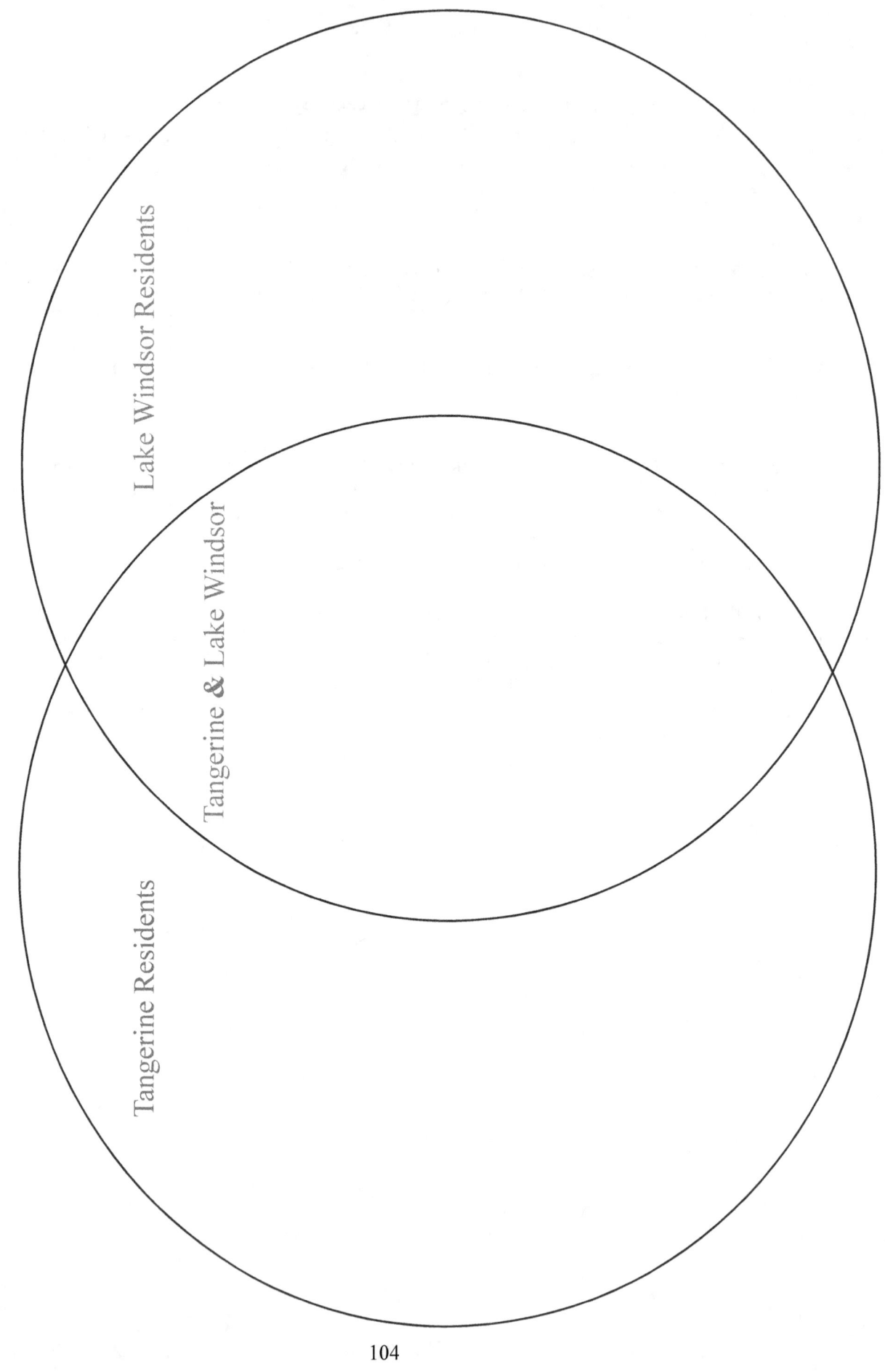

LESSON FIFTEEN

Objectives
1. To write to inform
2. To evaluate students' writing skills

Activity

Distribute the RAFT writing assignment to students. Explain that the purpose of this assignment is to write to inform. Tell students that they should select one of the scenarios listed for their third writing assignment. Explain that the "R" stands for the role they will take, or the point of view they are writing from; the "A" stands for the audience they are writing to; the "F" stands for the format of their writing; and the "T" stands for the topic or task. Quickly go over the different scenarios available to them and give the remaining time for students to complete the assignment.

Note: As students complete this writing assignment, call individuals up for writing conferences on the past two writing assignments. Use the evaluation form to guide you in your conference.

Tangerine Writing Assignment – RAFT

Directions: Select one of the following writing situations to use as the topic for your essay.

Role *The voice you take on as a writer; this is the perspective you are writing from*	Audience *Who you are writing to; this is the person that will be reading what you write*	Format *The form your writing will take; this is the type of writing you will complete*	Topic/Task *Your purpose for writing; this is the content or reason for your writing assignment*
Paul	His parents	Letter	Explaining how you've felt growing up with Erik and how you feel about their decision not to tell you what really happened to your eyesight
Mr. Donnelly (the newspaper journalist)	The people of Lake Windsor Downs	Newspaper Article	Article for readers in Lake Windsor Downs to open their eyes about the lives of those in Tangerine
Scientist	The Public	Speech	How nature and the environment of an area can have an affect on the lives of residents
Person with a physical disability	A child with a disability	Email	How to overcome being different and enjoy living an active life

WRITING ASSIGNMENT #3 – *Tangerine*
Writing to Inform

PROMPT
Select one of the scenarios listed on the RAFT writing assignment for the topic of your essay. The role is the point of view you are writing from, the audience is who you are writing to, the format is the type of writing you are doing, and the topic/task is the actual information you are writing about.

PREWRITING
Once you have selected your writing scenario, begin to brainstorm ideas. Remember to think about the role you are writing from and the topic you are writing about. Use your book, notes from the speaker, and notes from the non-fiction articles to help you with your support.

DRAFTING
Write an introductory paragraph that allows the reader to know the role you have assumed and the audience you are writing to. Give a general overview of the points you will make in the body paragraphs of your writing. Use the format of your writing to guide you on how to begin (speech would begin with a little about yourself, letter begins with Dear _____, etc).

In the body paragraphs, give the details of your topic. Use information from the novel, the speaker, and the non-fiction article you read to help provide support. Be sure to reread the topic/task you are writing on and be sure to cover all portions listed there.

In your conclusion paragraph, summarize your main points and conclude the writing assignment. For unity with your writing, you may want to tie in your role and audience once again.

PROMPT
When you finish the rough draft of your composition, ask a student who sits near you to read it. After reading your rough draft, he/she should tell you what he/she liked best about your work, which parts were difficult to understand, and ways in which your work could be improved. Reread your paper considering your critic's comments, and make the corrections you think are necessary. Ask your classmate what he/she thought of each of the characters/events you chose for your assignment.

PROOFREADING
Do a final proofreading of your paper double-checking your grammar, spelling, organization, and the clarity of your ideas.

LESSONS SIXTEEN AND SEVENTEEN

<u>Objectives</u>
1. To discuss the novel on a deeper than direct-recall level
2. To prepare students for questions and topics convered on the test
3. To make personal connections with the text
4. To give students the opportunity to share their projects with the class

<u>Activity 1</u>
Choose the questions from the Extra Discussion Questions/Writing Assignments which seem most appropriate for your students. A class discussion of these questions is most effective if students have been given the opportunity to formulate answers to the questions prior to the discussion. To this end, you may either have all the students formulate answers to all the questions, divide your class into groups and assign one or more questions to each group, or you could assign one question to each student in your class. The option you choose will make a difference in the amount of class time needed for this activity.

Note: The use of graphic organizers may be helpful to students in preparing their answers. Encourage them to use any diagrams or graphics that they feel are necessary.

<u>Activity 2</u>
After reviewing the extra discussion questions, collect the Environmental Study Project assigned to students on the first day of the unit. Allow students the opportunity to share their projects with the class. You may need additional time to complete this activity.

EXTRA DISCUSSION QUESTIONS/WRITING ASSIGNMENTS *Tangerine*

Interpretive
1. How does Paul feel about Erik's football career? Use evidence from the text to support your answer.
2. How does Erik regard his brother's vision problem?
3. What metaphor does Paul use to describe his old house?
4. From what point of view is the story told? Why is that important?
5. What is the setting, and what does it add to the story?
6. Describe the author's writing style. Give specific examples to support your answer.
7. What are two main conflicts in the story? Are they resolved? If so, how? If not, why not?
8. How does the author use foreshadowing in the story? Give at least one example.
9. In what genre would you classify this book? Why?
10. How do flashbacks enhance the story?
11. How is the new development Paul and his family live in contradicting nature? What problems is the neighborhood having as a result of destroying the original land to build houses?
12. After Tino beats up Erik he says, "That's for Luis Cruz! I take care of his light work." Of what literary element is this an example?
13. Aside from the championship title, why is the soccer match against Lake Windsor so important? What else is at stake?
14. Compare and contrast the support at soccer games from the family and friends of Tangerine Middle School players with the family support from the players that transferred from Lake Windsor.
15. After Erik is humiliated on the local news for his fake kick in the first football game, Paul says, "Erik can't laugh this off. Erik can't leave this humiliation behind him. Someone has to pay for this. I'm not sure why I'm sure. But I am. Someone has to pay for this." Of what literary element is this an example?
16. Paul is worried that the guys on his new team will find out he was the one who told on them about the vandalism. How does he get away with it?
17. Describe how the sinkhole disaster affected every person in Paul's family.
18. Joey tells Paul that the kids on the Tangerine Middle School soccer team have guns and are in gangs. How does this compare to the type of kids who are on the Lake Windsor Middle School soccer team?
19. Where does Paul hear about how his eyes became damaged? What evidence does he have to believe the story? Why does he doubt the story?
20. Describe how Paul and his mother first feel about the town of Tangerine. What discoveries do the two make that make them weary of the town?
21. List five of Paul's most important character traits and give examples of each.

Critical
22. How does Paul regard his father's relationship with Erik?
23. Compare and contrast the way Florida really looks with the Florida Paul pictured in his mind.
24. Describe the predator and prey metaphor Paul uses in his first flashback.

25. Choose four events in the book and explain how each one helped Paul grow a little more.
26. *The Bulletin* said that Tangerine is "a richly imagined read about an underdog coming into his own." Defend that statement using the text for support.
27. How is the theme of things not being what they seem on the outside portrayed throughout the novel? Give multiple examples from the text to support your answer.
28. What statement does this book make about the role of nature in society?
29. What point was the author trying to make about the differences between the wealthy and the working class? How does he illustrate his point throughout the novel?
30. What role does the scent of a golden dawn play in the novel? Describe the multiple ways it is used throughout the text.
31. Explain what Paul means when he says, "Mike Costello has his tree, and that's good. But Luis has his tree, too, and he will have many, many more."
32. Paul says, "There's no big mystery here. The truth about Luis is obvious to all the people around him. Their lives are not made up of bits and pieces and versions of the truth. They don't live that way. They know what really happened. Period. Why would that seem so mysterious to me?" What does Paul mean when he says this? How are the lives different for those in Tangerine and those in Lake Windsor Downs when it comes to facing the truth? Use examples from the text to support your answer.
33. Why is soccer so important to Paul? Why is he so emotional after the championship win?
34. Paul says, "It was strange. Very strange. I was driving past the sights that made up my ride to and from school, every day. But today I looked at them through the hostile eyes of a War Eagle." Why is this drive different for Paul? How do you think he feels about the neighborhood that is different than his teammates? What striking difference in background does this ride point out?
35. At times Paul denies he has a handicap and thinks he is just like everyone else. When it comes to girls, he feels like a freak that should travel with the carnival. Why do you think his self confidence changes so much? What situations does he feel good about himself? What other situations make him feel bad about himself?
36. Paul observes that Arthur's life is about to change all because of Erik. Arthur was a nobody at school, yet after becoming friends with Erik, Paul knows that somehow he will become a star. He says, "What will Arthur do for an opportunity like that, for that kind of fame and glory? What will Arthur do for Erik, his sponsor, his benefactor, his ticket to the big time? Let's face it. He will do anything. He will do anything that Erik asks." Why do you think someone as popular as Erik makes friends with someone like Arthur? Why wouldn't Erik make friends with the others stars like Antoine or Mike?
37. Paul thinks one night, "Erik's arrival is going to change the football season...Dad's arrival is going to change how things are done in the Civil Engineering Department...Mom's arrival will change the Homeowner's Association...so what about me?" What does this reveal about Paul's views of his role in the family?
38. How does the reader know that Luis's creation, the Golden Dawn Tangerine, is going to be a success?
39. How does Paul's dad's attitude towards Erik change once police begin to investigate him for Luis's murder?

40. After Paul goes on a shopping spree with his mom he goes home and puts away his new clothes that fit. What do these new clothes symbolize?
41. As Paul walks out of Tangerine Middle School after being suspended, how do the other kids act? Why do they act like this?
42. How does the reader know that Tino has respect for Joey Costello?
43. Why is Theresa upset at Paul for coming to her school, working at her house, and jumping on the coach?
44. When Paul's grandparents arrive his grandpop looks at Erik's face and says, "What the hell happened to your eyes?" How is this an example of irony?
45. Why do the homeowners ultimately decide to give Erik and Arthur a second chance?
46. The Fishers and the Bauers try to come to an agreement with the owners of the homes that were broken into so that Erik and Arthur won't be prosecuted and have this mistake on their permanent record. Compare and contrast the arguments of the Fishers and the Bauers with the arguments of the other homeowners over what to do.
47. Why do the people of Lake Windsor Downs allow Antoine to play football on their team, knowing that he lives in Tangerine? How do those same people react when the Tangerine County Sports Commission nullifies all of the victories and records of the team?
48. Describe the metaphor Mr. Donnelly uses in his article entitled "Thoughts on an Imaginary Porcelain Plate." What is the point of this article?
49. In what ways does Antoine assist in the destruction of Erik's life?
50. Why does Paul pass out as he looks at the vandalism on the perimeter wall? How does his dad react? Why does he react this way?
51. Antoine lied about his address to play for a better team and hopefully be recruited for college football. How did this lie end up affecting his sister? How did it affect others in the community?
52. How has Paul used the knowledge gained in his flashbacks to grow as an individual?
53. How do Paul's parents react when he confronts them about how he went blind? What does this say about how the truth has affected them all this time?
54. Where does Paul find his strength? What changes in his life that erases his fear of Erik?
55. Paul says, "That shot from the blackjack had been just as deadly to Luis as a shot from a gun." What does he mean? How is being hit from a blackjack as bad as being shot?
56. Why do you think no one woke Paul up for Thanksgiving dinner after the last football game?
57. Compare and contrast the freeze in Tangerine with the freeze in Lake Windsor Downs. What does this say about the people from both locations?
58. Why doesn't Paul tell his parents about Arthur using a deadly weapon to hit Luis? Why doesn't Luis say anything to the police?
59. How does Erik use Arthur? Does he really value his friendship? What role does Arthur play in Erik's life?

60. Paul's mother has to go to a conference over Erik's slipping grades. She says it's normal for athletes to slip academically during game season. Paul points out, "I'm an athlete. A champion athlete, in fact. And I didn't slack off during the season." Why does his mother allow Erik to slip but pay no attention to Paul's success?

61. Why doesn't Paul tell his mom about Erik's punching Tino? Why doesn't he tell her about Arthur using a blackjack and nearly knocking out Luis?

62. Paul sees something flash in the window after Erik punches Tino. He suspects it was his father watching the whole time. Why doesn't Paul say something to him about what happened? Why would his father ignore Erik hurting someone the way he did?

63. Paul says, "Today was the day when the science group came over to my house. I guess it was a big deal for me. I had never had anybody over to the house except Joey, and who knows if that'll happen again." Why doesn't Paul have people from school over to his house more often?

64. What does Paul mean when he says that the soccer games they play are like war?

65. How does Tino react when he discovers Paul was the one who got him suspended for vandalizing the exhibit at the carnival? Why does he act the way he does?

66. How does Luis create new varieties of tangerines? How could this detail be important?

67. Joey feels like he's "learning to live among the natives" at Tangerine Middle School. Paul responds by thinking, "I took in the ugliness of Joey's words, and I saw, for the first time, how different he was from me." Why is Paul fitting in at school better than Joey? What is Paul doing right? What is Joey doing wrong?

68. The Tangerine Times comes to soccer practice to do a feature on the girl soccer players. When the paper is printed there is no story, only a picture of Nita being called Maya in the caption. Why is this significant?

69. How does Erik's personality change when he is in front of his mom? Why is this?

70. Tangerine Middle School is full of minorities. Why does Paul feel more comfortable there?

71. How is Tangerine Middle School different than Lake Windsor Middle school?

72. What type of relationship does Paul have with his dad? Use examples from the text to support your answer.

73. What do Paul's actions during the sinkhole disaster say about his character?

74. On the day of Mike's funeral, the football coach still holds practice. Compare and contrast the way Paul's mother feels about this practice with the way his father feels.

75. Why is it so important to Paul that his mother believes his vision has improved?

76. Why is Paul insulted about being given the position of team manager?

77. After Erik tells his mother the story of Mike's death he heads to the backyard with his friends. Paul watches his brother and is shocked to hear them making fun of the way Mike looked when he died and joking about the whole situation. What does this say about Erik's character?

78. Compare and contrast the way Paul feels about his vision problem with the way his mother feels.

Critical/Personal Response

79. Who was responsible for Luis's death? Defend your answer using specific information from the text.

80. If social services had been aware of Paul's home situation and the truth about everything, do you think they would have put Paul in a foster home? Justify your answer using specific examples from the text.

81. Would you say the people and events in *Tangerine* are extraordinary or more universal? Defend your choice with examples from the text.

82. The back of the book *Tangerine* says, "Welcome to Tangerine. This place is weirder than it looks." Do you agree with that statement? Using the text for support, defend your poisition.

83. In writing a statement for the police Paul says, "I started with the basic facts, a paragraph or two, but I couldn't stop there. I had too much to say. I started writing about Luis, and what he meant to the people around him, and how they depended on him, and why they looked up to him. Then I tried to write the same thing about Erik: What did he mean to the people around him? How did they depend on him? Why did they look up to him?" What do you suppose he wrote about Luis? How did he answer those same questions for Erik?

84. What do you think is wrong with Erik? What do you think could be done to help him?

85. As Paul's parents are explaining the robberies and murder charges Erik is involved with Paul reflects, "Grandmom and Grandpop didn't seem surprised by any of what they heard. They took it all in without even blinking." Why do you think his grandparents were so calm in hearing this news?

86. When confronted about a deal to prevent homeowners of the stolen goods from pressing charges against Erik and Arthur one person says, "Why should they escape all punishment for their crimes? That's not justice. What if the cops nabbed two kids from Tangerine for robbing our houses? They'd be in jail by now." Do you agree with this statement? Why or why not? Use details from the text to support your answer.

87. Paul's parents know Erik was the cause of Paul's blindness. They tell him the doctors thought he might never remember the truth, and to prevent him from hating his brother, they decided not to tell him what really happened. Do you think this was the right thing to do? How did it hurt Paul not to know the truth? How did it help Paul not to know the truth? Use details from the text to support your answer.

88. Were Tino and Victor right in showing up at the awards night to beat up Erik and Arthur? Justify your answer. If you were Tino, how would you have handled the situation?

89. Erik misses all five extra-point kicks at the last football game. Who does his Dad blame for these mistakes? Do you think the bad snaps were intentional? Explain why or why not.

90. What does Paul's mom think when she picks him up from battling the freeze? What story does he give her? Do you think she believes him?

91. Luis tells Paul he is going to get revenge with Erik. Paul thinks, "How could I be so totally afraid, and Luis be not the slightest bit afraid, of the exact same thing? Which one of us saw it wrong?" Who do you think is wrong? Should Luis be afraid of Erik? Should Paul be afraid of Erik? Explain your answer using details from the text.

92. Victor and other people help Tino's family during the freeze. Why do they volunteer to help? When have you ever done something that was difficult to help out a friend?

93. Why does Paul's mother sit on the home side of the soccer field even though her son is on the visitor side? If you were in her position, where would you sit?
94. Tino and Joey start to fight when Joey insults Luis and the new fruit he has worked so hard to create. Do you think it is fair that only Tino gets suspended? What does this say about the school?
95. Why is Paul so excited that Kerri might like him? Have you ever felt this way?
96. How does Paul have to prove himself to the soccer team at Tangerine? Also, give an example of a time in your life when you had to prove yourself to someone.
97. Paul's mom points out that Tangerine County is the lightning strike capital of the United States and that lightning is the top cause for accidental death in the area. Despite this knowledge, very few people in the area seem to fear lighting or take any extra caution in staying safe. Why do you think this is? Also, give an example of something dangerous you know of that not many people take seriously.
98. Paul's mother wants football practice to be moved to the morning to prevent another lightning strike death. The coach wants to keep practice the way it is. Compare and contrast the two viewpoints and decide which you think is best and tell why.

Personal Response

99. Paul's grandpop sneaks up to Erik's room and says a few words to him before leaving. Give an example of a time you made a mistake where someone talked to you about what you did.
100. Shandra tells Paul, "That kind of lie eats away at people, day by day, till it makes them sick at heart. And that's why Antoine didn't show up to collect any awards last night. He was feeling sick at heart." Have you ever been involved in a lie that made you feel this way?
101. If you were Paul's parents, what would you have done about Erik's damaging his brother's vision?
102. A lot of people in the novel want to take revenge on others. Do you think revenge is a good idea? When have you ever wanted to seek revenge on someone? Did you follow through with it? Why or why not? Looking back, was it the right decision?
103. Paul tells the little boy by the pond that his parents tell him lies and stories to keep him scared. What stories did your parents tell you? Why do you think they told you those stories? Would you do the same to your children?
104. When Paul volunteered to help Tino's family, he revealed a lot about his character. What have you done to prove who you really are deep down inside?
105. Paul begins to cry after the bus ride home from the championship game. The feeling of being part of something so significant meant a lot to him. Talk about a time in your life when you were a part of something huge and felt proud of your contribution.
106. Paul has a genuine interest in his tangerine project. Give an example of something you learned in school that really sparked your interest.
107. Erik and Arthur make fun of Mike's death in front of Joey. Afterwards, Paul says to Joey, "He's no Mike Costello. Nowhere near. He doesn't have the talent. He doesn't have the character. So what's he going to do? He's going to mock him. He's going to put him down." Why do people feel the need to make fun of others and put them down? Talk about a time in your life when you have seen this happen.
108. Paul feels like his dad pays more attention to his brother. Do you ever feel like your parents or family favor one child over another? Explain your answer.

109. Paul watches as Joey tries to handle the death of his brother. He feels sorry for him and the rest of his family during this difficult time. How have you had to deal with death in your life? How have you helped comfort others when they trying to deal with the loss of a loved one?

110. Paul has some unique ideas about lightning remembering and knowing things. Others laugh at him, but in a way, his thoughts make sense. Do you agree with Paul's reasoning of lightning having a memory of the land before the development, or do you think the weather is all a coincidence? Explain your answer.

111. Paul has one set of grandparents on his mother's side of the family. He says his mother rarely mentions them and it seems they are not very close. Describe the relationship you have with your grandparents and how that impacts your life.

112. Paul thinks Florida will be all sand and beaches. When he gets there, he sees it doesn't quite live up to the stereotype in his mind. What do people think about the place where you live? How does the reality of where you live differ from what people usually think when they hear where you live?

113. Paul thinks football is boring and a lot less work than soccer. He views soccer as a more challenging sport for athletes. What sport do you feel is the most challenging? Why?

114. Paul gets kicked off the soccer team because of his handicap, even though he is one of the best players on the field. Do you think the school has the right to kick him off the team due to insurance purposes? Explain your answer.

115. What does Paul mean when he says, "But I can see. I can see everything. I can see things that Mom and Dad can't. Or won't."? Also, describe a time in your life where you have seen things that your parents can't or won't see.

Quotations Tangerine *Tangerine*

1. An old familiar feeling came over me, like I had forgotten something. What was it? What did I need to remember? (Introduction)

2. Erik Fisher's younger brother, Eclipse Boy, visually impaired and totally incapable of following in his brother's footsteps. (Monday, August 28)

3. I've always been afraid of Erik. Now I get to be afraid of Erik and Arthur. (Wednesday, August 30)

4. What if Erik was the body at the undertaker's now? How would I feel about that? I would feel relieved. But I would feel sorry, too. Erik is a part of that eclipse story. I know he is. Erik is a part of whatever it is that I need to remember. I don't want Erik to die and take his part of the story with him. (Wednesday, September 6)

5. I'm sorry, but there is no way we can justify putting a visually handicapped student in the goal, of all places, where he could get his head kicked in. (Friday, September 8)

6. "Paul, all I can do is apologize, and promise that I'll never mention your eyesight to anyone ever again." I was too hurt and angry to tell her that I appreciated those words. That those words helped. But they did. (Friday, September 8)

7. I remembered the face of the Boy Who Never Grew, the face of that eighty-nine-year-old little boy. I remembered the fear in his eyes. I know that fear. It's my fear. They may as well stick me in there [the freak show] with him. (Saturday, September 9)

8. The portables themselves were starting to break apart and move. The kids came diving out, jamming in the doorways, pushing into the back of other kids, knocking each other flat on the disintegrating boardwalk. They knocked each other into the moving mudslide that was now circling around them. I looked and saw the entire portable being swallowed up by the mud, its roof now where the porch steps should be. Joey and I dug our heels into the mud about halfway down to the bottom of the hole. We pulled and grabbed at kids as they made their way up the slippery incline to the top. I lost my balance twice and fell into the mud, but I managed to right myself quickly. My glasses were so caked with mud that I could no longer see anything clearly. I must have pulled twenty kids up. The whooshing sound was getting louder, and I felt afraid for the first time, afraid that we might all get sucked down and drown in the mud. (Monday, September 11)

9. I faced down danger today, maybe even death. When disaster struck, we all had to do something. In a way, we all had to become someone. I'm not saying I was a hero. All I did was slide around in the mud and try to pull people up. But I didn't panic and run, either. I'm still afraid of Erik. I'm afraid of Arthur now, too. But today I wasn't a coward, and that counts for something. (Monday, September 11, Later)

10. But that's Dad. You're either at the center of his world, or you're nowhere. There is no in-between. (Thursday, September 14)

11. Football season and soccer season happen at the same time, Dad. It's OK with me if you can't pay attention to both. (Friday, September 15)

12. At Tangerine Middle, the minorities are the majority. I have no problem with that. I've always felt like a minority because of my eyes. (Monday, September 18)

13. Why isn't my mother here? Or my father? They could be watching this game. So could Joey's parents. If we were playing football, they'd all be here. (Tuesday, September 26)

14. Kerri Gardner knows about my glasses, but she doesn't think there's anything wrong with me. (Tuesday, September 26, Later)

15. From that day on, I could see things that they [Paul's parents] could not. I could see Erik posing in front of them, in the shining light of the Football Dream. And I could see Erik lurking behind me, in the shadows of the clock. (Thursday, October 5)

16. Everyone in Tangerine County knows him [Erik] now. Or they think they do. (Thursday, November 2)

17. They were all sincerely amazed at this stretch of road, this stretch that I took for granted. It was like a movie--like a movie set, anyway--painted on plywood and propped up by two-by-fours. As phony as an Erik Fisher football hero smile. (Friday, November 10)

18. Mars, you were in my head on that shot. You made me miss. You made me choke. (Friday, November 10)

19. "Well, that was quite a ride." I swallowed hard and managed to say, "It sure was, Mom. It was quite a ride." (Friday, November 10)

20. Why couldn't I tell my own parents about Erik? What was wrong with me? What was wrong with all of us? (Tuesday, November 21)

21. Erik is a psycho, Mom. Do you really not know that? (Tuesday, November 21)

22. Arthur reached Luis, turned, and whipped the blackjack around with a loud whack against the side of Luis's head. Luis's arms shot up to cover his head as he staggered to the right and fell on one knee. Arthur stuck the blackjack back into his gym bag and continued walking, as if nothing had happened. Erik walked quickly past Luis. He explained, for the benefit of his group, "Arthur takes care of all my light work." (Tuesday, November 21)

23. In Lake Windsor Downs, the people were inside, welcoming the freeze with hot cocoa and fake logs and Christmas CDs. In Tangerine, the people were heading out to fight it with shovels and axes and burning tires. (Thursday, November 23)

24. I drifted back inside, thinking about my fear of Erik. How could I be so totally afraid, and Luis be not the slightest bit afraid, of the exact same thing? Which one of us is wrong? (Thursday, November 23)

25. "How many games did I play in, Dad?" He pulled back. "I don't know." "What position did I play when I did get into a game?" "How am I supposed to know that?" "OK. Here's one: How many field goals did Erik kick this year?" He stared at me, and then he blinked rapidly. "All right. Your point is taken." (Friday, November 24)

26. The whole truth is-- I feel very weird. But I can't say why. I can't remember why. (Friday, November 24)

27. Luis had been killed by Arthur Bauer on Tuesday, but it had taken six days for him to die. That shot from the blackjack had been just as deadly to Luis as a shot from a gun. (Tuesday, November 28)

28. There they stood--Tino and Victor. It was like a mirage. It was impossible. They couldn't be there. And yet they were. They were standing together on the sideline staring straight ahead, hard-eyed, totally focused, like the wrath of God. (Friday, December 1)

29. Then Tino, his voice trembling with rage and choked with tears, shouted, "That's for Luis Cruz! I take care of his light work." (Friday, December 1)

30. I understood that I was supposed to be terrified by this spectacle--these two demonic creatures on this dark, lonely road. But for once in my life, I wasn't. (Friday, December 1)

31. And I remembered Erik's fingers prying my eyelids open while Vincent Castor sprayed white paint into them. They left me screaming and rolling around on the floor of the garage. (Friday, December 1)

32. "Let me ask you one thing, Mom. When you got home from the hospital that day, did you see the white paint on Erik's hands?" She didn't hesitate. "Yes." "Did you know what happened?" "Yes." No one spoke for a couple of minutes. (Friday, December 1)

33. "We wanted to find a way to keep you from always hating your brother." I answered, "So you figured it would be better if I just hated myself?" (Friday, December 1)

34. Don't spend your life hiding under the bleachers, little brother. The truth shall set you free. (Saturday, December 2)

35. I stood up straight and faced them all, like I had seen Luis do. "I saw-- heard Erik Fisher tell him to do it." (Sunday, December 3, Later)

36. Do you realize, Mom, that I've never been anything but a nerd? And now I'm going to enter this nerd school, not as a fellow nerd, but as a feared and notorious outlaw? (Monday, December 4)

37. I started with the basic facts, a paragraph or two, but I couldn't stop there. I had too much to say. I started writing about Luis, and what he meant to the people around him, and how they depended on him, and why they looked up to him. Then I tried to write the same thing about Erik: What did he mean to the people around him? How did they depend on him? Why did they look up to him? I don't suppose the police are interested in all of that. That's not their job. But it's a part of the truth. A big part. And as Antoine Thomas told me, "The truth shall set you free." (Tuesday, December 5, Later)

LESSON EIGHTEEN

Objectives
To review all of the vocabulary work done in the unit

Activity
Choose one (or more) of the vocabulary review activities listed below and spend your class period as directed in the activity. Some of the materials for these review activities are located in the Vocabulary Resource Materials section in this LitPlan.

VOCABULARY REVIEW ACTIVITIES

1. Divide your class into two teams and have an old-fashioned spelling or definition bee.

2. Give each of your students (or students in groups of two, three or four) a *Tangerine* Vocabulary Word Search Puzzle. The person (group) to find all of the vocabulary words in the puzzle first wins.

3. Give students a *Tangerine* Vocabulary Word Search Puzzle without the word list. The person or group to find the most vocabulary words in the puzzle wins.

4. Use a *Tangerine* Vocabulary Crossword Puzzle. Put the puzzle onto a transparency on the overhead projector (so everyone can see it), and do the puzzle together as a class.

5. Give students a *Tangerine* Vocabulary Matching Worksheet to do.

6. Divide your class into two teams. Use *Tangerine* vocabulary words with their letters jumbled as a word list. Student 1 from Team A faces off against Student 1 from Team B. You write the first jumbled word on the board. The first student (1A or 1B) to unscramble the word wins the chance for his/her team to score points. If 1A wins the jumble, go to student 2A and give him/her a definition. He/she must give you the correct spelling of the vocabulary word which fits that definition. If he/she does, Team A scores a point, and you give student 3A a definition for which you expect a correctly spelled matching vocabulary word. Continue giving Team A definitions until some team member makes an incorrect response. An incorrect response sends the game back to the jumbled-word face off, this time with students 2A and 2B. Instead of repeating giving definitions to the first few students of each team, continue with the student after the one who gave the last incorrect response on the team. For example, if Team B wins the jumbled-word face-off, and student 5B gave the last incorrect answer for Team B, you would start this round of definition questions with student 6B, and so on. The team with the most points wins!

7. Have students write a story in which they correctly use as many vocabulary words as possible. Have students read their compositions orally! Post the most original compositions on your bulletin board!

LESSON NINETEEN

Objectives
To review the main ideas and events from the book

Activity
Choose one of the review games/activities suggested in this unit and spend your class time as directed there.

REVIEW GAMES/ACTIVITIES *Tangerine*

1. Ask the class to make up a unit test for *Tangerine*. The test should have 4 sections: matching, true/false, short answer, and essay. Students may use 1/2 period to make the test and then swap papers and use the other 1/2 class period to take a test a classmate has devised. (open book) You may want to use the unit test included in this packet or take questions from the students' unit tests to formulate your own test.

2. Take 1/2 period for students to make up true and false questions (including the answers). Collect the papers and divide the class into two teams. Draw a big tic-tac-toe board on the chalk board. Make one team X and one team O. Ask questions to each side, giving each student one turn. If the question is answered correctly, that students' team's letter (X or O) is placed in the box. If the answer is incorrect, no letter is placed in the box. The object is to get three in a row like tic-tac-toe. You may want to keep track of the number of games won for each team.

3. Take 1/2 period for students to make up questions (true/false and short answer). Collect the questions. Divide the class into two teams. You'll alternate asking questions to individual members of teams A & B (like in a spelling bee). The question keeps going from A to B until it is correctly answered, then a new question is asked. A correct answer does not allow the team to get another question. Correct answers are +2 points; incorrect answers are -1 point.

4. Have students pair up and quiz each other from their study guides and class notes.

5. Give students a *Tangerine* crossword puzzle to complete.

6. Play What's My Line?. This is similar to the old television show. Students assume the roles of different characters from the epic. One student gives clues to the class, or to a panel of contestants. The contestants try to guess the identity of the guest. Students may enjoy assisting you in creating rules and procedures for the game.

7. Divide your class into two teams. Use *Tangerine* crossword words with their letters jumbled as a word list. Student 1 from Team A faces off against Student 1 from Team B. You write the first jumbled word on the board. The first student (1A or 1B) to unscramble the word wins the chance for his/her team to score points. If 1A wins the jumble, go to student 2A and give him/her a clue. He/she must give you the correct word which matches that clue. If he/she does, Team A scores a point, and you give student 3A a clue for which you expect another correct response. Continue giving Team A clues until some team member makes an incorrect response. An incorrect response sends the game back to the jumbled-word face off, this time with students 2A and 2B. Instead of repeating giving clues to the first few students of each team, continue with the student after the one who gave the last incorrect response on the team. For example, if Team B wins the jumbled-word face-off, and student 5B gave the last incorrect answer for Team B, you would start this round of clue questions with student 6B, and so on. The team with the most points wins!

8. Play Jeopardy. Divide the class into two groups. Assign each group a category or book from the novel and have them devise answers for that category. Play the game according to the television show procedures.

9. Play Drawing in the Details. This is similar to Pictionary. Divide students into teams. A student from one team draws a scene from the novel. (You may want to specify the Book or section.) Drawings should be kept simple, to keep the pace lively. Students in the opposing team locate the scene in their books and read it aloud. If they are incorrect, the illustrator's team has a chance to guess. Involve students in setting up a scoring system and any other necessary rules.

10. Take students to a school soccer field. Divide students into two teams. Have student A from team 1 answer a question. If he/she gets it correct, he/she can take a free kick for an extra point. Next, allow student B from team 2 to answer a question. If the answer is correct he/she can take a free kick for a bonus point. Continue to ask questions awarding one point for a correct answer and one bonus point for a goal. Point out that part of the reason for the review is based on Paul's interest and talent in soccer.

LESSON TWENTY

Objectives
To evaluate the students' understanding of the main ideas, themes, events, and vocabulary in *Tangerine*

Activity 1
Distribute the unit tests, give students ample time to complete them, and collect the tests when students finish. Remember to collect assigned books prior to the end o the class period.

NOTE: There are 5 different unit tests included in the LitPlan Teacher Pack. Two are short answer, two are multiple choice. There is one advanced short answer test. The answers to the advanced short answer test will be based on the discussions you have had during class and should be graded accordingly. You should choose the tests and/or test parts which best suit your needs. Matching and short answer tests have answer keys. For essay type questions, grade according to your own criteria based on class discussions and the level of your students. Also, you will need to choose vocabulary words to read orally for the vocabulary section of the short answer tests.

UNIT TESTS

Tangerine Short Answer Unit Test 1

I. Matching/Identify

____ 1.	FLORIDA	A.	Person who pulls the ball away from Erik as he goes to kick for a last minute play
____ 2.	KERRI	B.	Theresa, Tino, and ___ all work with Paul on a school project.
____ 3.	SINKHOLE	C.	Paul's sport
____ 4.	SHOES	D.	Starts a fight with Joey over a comment he made about Luis
____ 5.	ARTHUR	E.	Antoine's little sister who plays on Paul's soccer team
____ 6.	MARS	F.	State where Paul and his family move at the start of the novel
____ 7.	FISHER	G.	Luis hurts his leg permanently from falling out of one.
____ 8.	THERESA	H.	Joey tries to take these off of his brother.
____ 9.	JOEY	I.	Does severe damage to Lake Windsor Middle School
____ 10.	ANTOINE	J.	Transfers to Tangerine Middle School & hates it
____ 11.	TREE	K.	Erik's sidekick
____ 12.	TINO	L.	Paul's nickname at Tangerine
____ 13.	MOSQUITOES	M.	Side effect of soaking the fields in water to get rid of the fires
____ 14.	SHANDRA	N.	Paul gets ___ from school for his actions at the award ceremony.
____ 15.	HENRY	O.	Paul's nickname at Lake Windsor Downs
____ 16.	FUNERAL	P.	Shows Paul around school on the first day
____ 17.	EXPELLED	Q.	Girl who likes Paul
____ 18.	FOOTBALL	R.	His older brother gets all the attention of his parents.
____ 19.	SOCCER	S.	Paul is asked not to attend Luis's.
____ 20.	PAUL	T.	The Erik Fisher ___ Dream

II. Short Answer

1. What does Paul write in his statement for the police?

2. What excuse has Paul always given people about why his vision is so poor?

3. What is Lake Windsor Middle School's policy on how many kids can be on the soccer team?

4. How does Mike Costello die?

5. What do Paul and Joey do when they see the portables being swallowed up by the sinkhole?

6. Why does Paul want to go to Tangerine Middle School so badly?

7. Why is the whole town laughing at Erik after the first football game?

8. What are a few of the unique qualities about the Golden Dawn tangerine?

9. What happens in the last play of the Lake Windsor soccer game?

10. What does Paul see while hiding under the bleachers at football practice?

11. How does Luis die?

12. What does Paul do during Luis's funeral?

13. Paul remembers the true story of losing his eyesight. What really happened?

14. What agreement do the Fishers and the Bauers want their neighbors to agree to in regards to their stolen property?

15. How does Paul feel about getting special attention at school because of his visual handicap?

III. Composition
1. What does Paul mean when he says, "But I can see. I can see everything. I can see things that Mom and Dad can't. Or won't."?

IV. Quotations: Explain the importance and meaning of the following quotations:

1. "But that's Dad. You're either at the center of his world, or you're nowhere. There is no in-between. (Thursday, September 14)"

2. "Kerri Gardner knows about my glasses, but she doesn't think there's anything wrong with me. (Tuesday, September 26, Later)"

3. "Why couldn't I tell my own parents about Erik? What was wrong with me? What was wrong with all of us? (Tuesday, November 21)"

4. ""We wanted to find a way to keep you from always hating your brother." I answered, "So you figured it would be better if I just hated myself?" (Friday, December 1)"

5. "Do you realize, Mom, that I've never been anything but a nerd? And now I'm going to enter this nerd school, not as a fellow nerd, but as a feared and notorious outlaw? (Monday, December 4)"

V. Vocabulary
   A. Write the vocabulary words you are given. After writing them down, go back and write in their definitions.

Word	Definition
1	
2	
3	
4	
5	
6	
7	
8	
9	
10	

   B. Write a short paragraph using 8 of these 10 words.

Tangerine Short Answer Unit Test 1 Answer Key

I. Matching/Identify

F	1.	FLORIDA	A.	Person who pulls the ball away from Erik as he goes to kick for a last minute play
Q	2.	KERRI	B.	Theresa, Tino, and ___ all work with Paul on a school project.
I	3.	SINKHOLE	C.	Paul's sport
H	4.	SHOES	D.	Starts a fight with Joey over a comment he made about Luis
K	5.	ARTHUR	E.	Antoine's little sister who plays on Paul's soccer team
O	6.	MARS	F.	State where Paul and his family move at the start of the novel
L	7.	FISHER	G.	Luis hurts his leg permanently from falling out of one.
P	8.	THERESA	H.	Joey tries to take these off of his brother.
J	9.	JOEY	I.	Does severe damage to Lake Windsor Middle School
A	10.	ANTOINE	J.	Transfers to Tangerine Middle School & hates it
G	11.	TREE	K.	Erik's sidekick
D	12.	TINO	L.	Paul's nickname at Tangerine
M	13.	MOSQUITOES	M.	Side effect of soaking the fields in water to get rid of the fires
E	14.	SHANDRA	N.	Paul gets ___ from school for his actions at the award ceremony.
B	15.	HENRY	O.	Paul's nickname at Lake Windsor Downs
S	16.	FUNERAL	P.	Shows Paul around school on the first day
N	17.	EXPELLED	Q.	Girl who likes Paul
T	18.	FOOTBALL	R.	His older brother gets all the attention of his parents.
C	19.	SOCCER	S.	Paul is asked not to attend Luis's.
R	20.	PAUL	T.	The Erik Fisher ___ Dream

II. Short Answer

1. What does Paul write in his statement for the police?
   He writes about what happened the day Luis was hit with the blackjack. He also writes about Luis and what he meant to the people around him. He talks about why people depended on him and how they looked up to him.

2. What excuse has Paul always given people about why his vision is so poor?
   Paul tells people he looked at an eclipse and it damaged his vision.

3. What is Lake Windsor Middle School's policy on how many kids can be on the soccer team?
   The school allows everyone who wants to be on the team to practice and get a uniform. No one gets cut from the team.

4. How does Mike Costello die?
   While leaning on the goalpost at football practice, he is struck by lightning and is killed immediately.

5. What do Paul and Joey do when they see the portables being swallowed up by the sinkhole?
   The two boys run and help rescue kids who are trapped in the portables.

6. Why does Paul want to go to Tangerine Middle School so badly?
   If he goes there, he can register without an IEP and will be eligible to play on the school soccer team.

7. Why is the whole town laughing at Erik after the first football game?
   As Erik went to kick the football, Antoine pulled it away for a two-point conversion. Erik didn't know what was happening and kicked at nothing, causing him to fly up in the air and land on his back in the mud. The local news played the clip and made fun of him that night.

8. What are a few of the unique qualities about the Golden Dawn tangerine?
   It is seedless, very juicy, and can withstand cold weather.

9. What happens in the last play of the Lake Windsor soccer game?
   Paul jumps the opposite way in the goal, missing where the ball is headed. Luckily, Gino is intimidated by Paul being in the goal and misses, tying the game. Since Lake Windsor has two ties and this is Tangerine's first, Tangerine wins the championship title.

10. What does Paul see while hiding under the bleachers at football practice?
    Paul sees Luis come to football practice looking for Erik. He confronts Erik about punching his brother. Arthur pulls a blackjack out of his bag and hits Luis in the head. He falls down and is hurt while Erik walks away laughing.

11. How does Luis die?
    He suffered from an aneurysm after being hit in the head. A blood clot formed after he was hit by Arthur, and it took six days for it to kill him.

12. What does Paul do during Luis's funeral?
    He pulls back a piece of sod and digs a hole. He puts his face near the hole and remembers Luis. He starts to cry while he thinks of Luis and then buries his tears in the hole.

13. Paul remembers the true story of losing his eyesight. What really happened?
    Erik and his friend Vincent Castor got in trouble for spray painting on a wall around the neighborhood where Paul and his family used to live. They assumed Paul was the one who told on them so Erik pinned Paul's arms behind his back and held open his eyelids while Vincent sprayed white paint into Paul's eyes.

14. What agreement do the Fishers and the Bauers want their neighbors to agree to in regards to their stolen property?
   They want their neighbors to not press charges against Erik and Arthur. Both families promise to return all of the stolen items or pay for the replacement of the stolen items if everyone will agree to give Erik and Arthur a second chance.

15. How does Paul feel about getting special attention at school because of his visual handicap?
   Paul is angry at his mother for bringing it to the attention of the school. He hates that his mom fills out a special plan for him and feels like he can see just fine.

Tangerine Short Answer Unit Test 2

I. Matching/Identify

____ 1. MUCK   A. Prevents Paul from playing soccer at LWD; later "disappears"
____ 2. GOGGLES   B. Tangerine's teams are known as the ___ Eagles.
____ 3. ECLIPSE   C. Paul wears these on his eyes while playing soccer.
____ 4. KERRI   D. Shows Paul around school on the first day
____ 5. SHOES   E. Girl who likes Paul
____ 6. ARTHUR   F. Paul's nickname at Lake Windsor Downs
____ 7. MARS   G. Former home of the Fisher family
____ 8. IEP   H. Starts a fight with Joey over a comment he made about Luis
____ 9. CARNIVAL   I. Theresa, Tino, and ___ all work with Paul on a school project.
____ 10. THERESA   J. Paul tells people he looked at an ___ for too long, causing damage to his eyes
____ 11. JOEY   K. Antoine's little sister who plays on Paul's soccer team
____ 12. WAR   L. Joey tries to take these off of his brother.
____ 13. ANTOINE   M. This type of fire is continuously burning behind Paul's house.
____ 14. DAWN   N. Erik's sidekick
____ 15. TINO   O. Luis creates a tangerine called the Golden ___.
____ 16. SHANDRA   P. Paul's mom finds the stolen goods in the ___ unit.
____ 17. HENRY   Q. Person who pulls the ball away from Erik as he goes to kick for a last minute play
____ 18. STORAGE   R. Paul rats out the Tangerine soccer players for vandalizing an exhibit at the ___.
____ 19. HOUSTON   S. Paul occasionally has these, about the past.
____ 20. FLASHBACKS   T. Transfers to Tangerine Middle School & hates it

II. Short Answer

1. What scene does Paul remember while he is waiting for his mother in the driveway of their old home?

2. Why does Paul have a hard time believing the story his brother told him about how he damaged his vision?

3. Why is Paul kicked off the soccer team?

4. What surprises both Paul and his mother about the Tangerine soccer team?

5. Why is the whole town laughing at Erik after the first football game?

6. What are a few of the unique qualities about the Golden Dawn tangerine?

7. What is happening to the houses that are tented for termites?

8. Why is the soccer game against Lake Windsor Middle School such a big deal?

9. What do Paul's grandparents think of "the Erik Fisher Football Dream"?

10. Why are so many kids absent from school the first day it is cold?

11. What are the people in Lake Windsor Downs doing while the people of Tangerine are doing back-breaking work in the cold to save their trees?

12. What does Paul do during Luis's funeral?

13. Paul confronts his parents about how he lost his eyesight. What excuse do they give him about not telling him the truth?

14. Why doesn't Shandra put her picture in the newspaper when she makes the All-County Middle School Soccer Team?

15. Why is Paul excited about going to St. Anthony's on a trial basis?

III. Composition
1. List five of Paul's most important character traits and give examples of each.

2. How does Erik use Arthur? Does he really value his friendship? What role does Arthur play in Erik's life?

IV. Quotations: Explain the importance and meaning of the following quotations:

1. ""Paul, all I can do is apologize, and promise that I'll never mention your eyesight to anyone ever again." I was too hurt and angry to tell her that I appreciated those words. That those words helped. But they did. (Friday, September 8)"

2. "I remembered the face of the Boy Who Never Grew, the face of that eighty-nine-year-old little boy. I remembered the fear in his eyes. I know that fear. It's my fear. They may as well stick me in there [the freak show] with him. (Saturday, September 9)"

3. "Football season and soccer season happen at the same time, Dad. It's OK with me if you can't pay attention to both. (Friday, September 15)"

4. "From that day on, I could see things that they [Paul's parents] could not. I could see Erik posing in front of them, in the shining light of the Football Dream. And I could see Erik lurking behind me, in the shadows of the clock. (Thursday, October 5)"

5. "Everyone in Tangerine County knows him [Erik] now. Or they think they do. (Thursday, November 2)"

6. "They were all sincerely amazed at this stretch of road, this stretch that I took for granted. It was like a movie--like a movie set, anyway--painted on plywood and propped up by two-by-fours. As phony as an Erik Fisher football hero smile. (Friday, November 10)"

7. ""How many games did I play in, Dad?" He pulled back. "I don't know." "What position did I play when I did get into a game?" "How am I supposed to know that?" "OK. Here's one: How many field goals did Erik kick this year?" He stared at me, and then he blinked rapidly. "All right. Your point is taken." (Friday, November 24)"

8. ""We wanted to find a way to keep you from always hating your brother." I answered, "So you figured it would be better if I just hated myself?" (Friday, December 1)"

9. "Do you realize, Mom, that I've never been anything but a nerd? And now I'm going to enter this nerd school, not as a fellow nerd, but as a feared and notorious outlaw? (Monday, December 4)"

10. "I started with the basic facts, a paragraph or two, but I couldn't stop there. I had too much to say. I started writing about Luis, and what he meant to the people around him, and how they depended on him, and why they looked up to him. Then I tried to write the same thing about Erik: What did he mean to the people around him? How did they depend on him? Why did they look up to him? I don't suppose the police are interested in all of that. That's not their job. But it's a part of the truth. A big part. And as Antoine Thomas told me, "The truth shall set you free." (Tuesday, December 5, Later)"

V. Vocabulary
   A. Write the vocabulary words you are given. After writing them down, go back and write in their definitions.

Word	Definition
1	
2	
3	
4	
5	
6	
7	
8	
9	
10	

   B. Write a short paragraph using 8 of these 10 words.

Tangerine Short Answer Unit Test 2 Answer Key

I. Matching/Identify

M	1.	MUCK	A.	Prevents Paul from playing soccer at LWD; later "disappears"
C	2.	GOGGLES	B.	Tangerine's teams are known as the ___ Eagles.
J	3.	ECLIPSE	C.	Paul wears these on his eyes while playing soccer.
E	4.	KERRI	D.	Shows Paul around school on the first day
L	5.	SHOES	E.	Girl who likes Paul
N	6.	ARTHUR	F.	Paul's nickname at Lake Windsor Downs
F	7.	MARS	G.	Former home of the Fisher family
A	8.	IEP	H.	Starts a fight with Joey over a comment he made about Luis
R	9.	CARNIVAL	I.	Theresa, Tino, and ___ all work with Paul on a school project.
D	10.	THERESA	J.	Paul tells people he looked at an ___ for too long, causing damage to his eyes
T	11.	JOEY	K.	Antoine's little sister who plays on Paul's soccer team
B	12.	WAR	L.	Joey tries to take these off of his brother.
Q	13.	ANTOINE	M.	This type of fire is continuously burning behind Paul's house.
O	14.	DAWN	N.	Erik's sidekick
H	15.	TINO	O.	Luis creates a tangerine called the Golden ___.
K	16.	SHANDRA	P.	Paul's mom finds the stolen goods in the ___ unit.
I	17.	HENRY	Q.	Person who pulls the ball away from Erik as he goes to kick for a last minute play
P	18.	STORAGE	R.	Paul rats out the Tangerine soccer players for vandalizing an exhibit at the ___.
G	19.	HOUSTON	S.	Paul occasionally has these, about the past.
S	20.	FLASHBACKS	T.	Transfers to Tangerine Middle School & hates it

II. Short Answer

1. What scene does Paul remember while he is waiting for his mother in the driveway of their old home?
   Paul remembers riding his bike when a car full of shouting teenagers came up behind him. Someone was hanging out the window with a baseball bat and slammed it into a mailbox right next to Paul's head. He was terrified and thought his brother Erik was trying to kill him.

2. Why does Paul have a hard time believing the story his brother told him about how he damaged his vision?
   Paul thinks that if the story is true, he should be able to remember it happening.

3. Why is Paul kicked off the soccer team?
   Since Paul's mother labeled him as handicapped with the school, he is not allowed to play on any sports team. The school's insurance company won't cover anyone who is already labeled as handicapped.

4. What surprises both Paul and his mother about the Tangerine soccer team?
   The team is a mix of girls and boys. The girls on the team are starters and the best players in the county.

5. Why is the whole town laughing at Erik after the first football game?
   As Erik went to kick the football, Antoine pulled it away for a two-point conversion. Erik didn't know what was happening and kicked at nothing, causing him to fly up in the air and land on his back in the mud. The local news played the clip and made fun of him that night.

6. What are a few of the unique qualities about the Golden Dawn tangerine?
   It is seedless, very juicy, and can withstand cold weather.

7. What is happening to the houses that are tented for termites?
   They are all being robbed.

8. Why is the soccer game against Lake Windsor Middle School such a big deal?
   Both teams are undefeated, so the team that wins will be the county champion.

9. What do Paul's grandparents think of "the Erik Fisher Football Dream"?
   They couldn't care less about Erik's football career. They change the subject anytime it comes up.

10. Why are so many kids absent from school the first day it is cold?
    The kids are all helping their families fight the freeze to keep their produce alive.

11. What are the people in Lake Windsor Downs doing while the people of Tangerine are doing back-breaking work in the cold to save their trees?
    The people of Lake Windsor Downs are making hot chocolate, lighting their fireplaces, and preparing for the Christmas season.

12. What does Paul do during Luis's funeral?
    He pulls back a piece of sod and digs a hole. He puts his face near the hole and remembers Luis. He starts to cry while he thinks of Luis and then buries his tears in the hole.

13. Paul confronts his parents about how he lost his eyesight. What excuse do they give him about not telling him the truth?
    Paul's parents tell him they didn't want him to hate his brother, and since the doctors said he might never remember what really happened, they decided not to tell him.

14. Why doesn't Shandra put her picture in the newspaper when she makes the All-County Middle School Soccer Team?
    Shandra is afraid to put her photo in the newspaper with the other kids in case someone recognizes that she is Antoine's little sister and figures out Antoine is playing for the wrong team.

15. Why is Paul excited about going to St. Anthony's on a trial basis?
    He knows he will have a bad reputation and kids will fear him. He has never been anything other than a nerd and is happy to be feared.

Tangerine Advanced Short Answer Unit Test

I. Matching

____ 1.	FLORIDA	A.	Cause of Luis's death
____ 2.	MUCK	B.	This type of fire is continuously burning behind Paul's house.
____ 3.	LIGHTNING	C.	State where Paul and his family move at the start of the novel
____ 4.	MUD	D.	Paul's nickname at Tangerine
____ 5.	KERRI	E.	Antoine's little sister who plays on Paul's soccer team
____ 6.	ARTHUR	F.	How Paul says he would feel if his brother died
____ 7.	MARS	G.	The houses tented for ___ were being robbed.
____ 8.	FISHER	H.	Paul's nickname at Lake Windsor Downs
____ 9.	THERESA	I.	Starts a fight with Joey over a comment he made about Luis
____ 10.	GIRLS	J.	Shows Paul around school on the first day
____ 11.	JOEY	K.	Kills Mike Castello
____ 12.	ANTOINE	L.	Person who pulls the ball away from Erik as he goes to kick for a last minute play
____ 13.	ANEURYSM	M.	Girl who likes Paul
____ 14.	BLACKJACK	N.	Arthur uses it to hit Luis.
____ 15.	TINO	O.	Paul & his mom are shocked to see *they* play on the soccer team.
____ 16.	TERMITES	P.	Theresa, Tino, and ___ all work with Paul on a school project.
____ 17.	SHANDRA	Q.	Erik's sidekick
____ 18.	HENRY	R.	Someone smears this in Paul's face, causing him to start a fight.
____ 19.	NULLIFIES	S.	The county ___ all LW victories in which Antoine played.
____ 20.	RELIEVED	T.	Transfers to Tangerine Middle School & hates it

II. Short Answer
1. How does the author use foreshadowing in the story? Give at least one example.

2. What are two main conflicts in the story? Are they resolved? If so, how? If not, why not?

3. How does Paul regard his father's relationship with Erik?

4. Where does Paul hear about how his eyes became damaged? What evidence does he have to believe the story? Why does he doubt the story?

5. What type of relationship does Paul have with his dad? Use examples from the text to support your answer.

6. Tangerine Middle School is full of minorities. Why does Paul feel more comfortable there?

7. What does Paul mean when he says that the soccer games they play are like war?

8. How does Erik use Arthur? Does he really value his friendship? What role does Arthur play in Erik's life?

9. Why do you think no one woke Paul up for Thanksgiving dinner after the last football game?

10. How do Paul's parents react when he confronts them about how he went blind? What does this say about how the truth has affected them all this time?

11. Why do the homeowners ultimately decide to give Erik and Arthur a second chance?

12. When Paul's grandparents arrive his grandpop looks at Erik's face and says, "What the hell happened to your eyes?" How is this an example of irony?

13. After Paul goes on a shopping spree with his mom he goes home and puts away his new clothes that fit. What do these new clothes symbolize?

14. Paul says, "It was strange. Very strange. I was driving past the sights that made up my ride to and from school, every day. But today I looked at them through the hostile eyes of a War Eagle." Why is this drive different for Paul? How do you think he feels about the neighborhood that is different than his teammates? What striking difference in background does this ride point out?

III. Essay

1. The back of the book *Tangerine* says, "Welcome to Tangerine. This place is weirder than it looks." Do you agree with that statement? Using the text for support, defend your poisition.

2. If social services had been aware of Paul's home situation and the truth about everything, do you think they would have put Paul in a foster home? Justify your answer using specific examples from the text.

IV. Quotations: Explain the importance and meaning of the following quotations:

1. "An old familiar feeling came over me, like I had forgotten something. What was it? What did I need to remember? (Introduction)"

2. "At Tangerine Middle, the minorities are the majority. I have no problem with that. I've always felt like a minority because of my eyes. (Monday, September 18)"

3. "Kerri Gardner knows about my glasses, but she doesn't think there's anything wrong with me. (Tuesday, September 26, Later)"

4. "From that day on, I could see things that they [Paul's parents] could not. I could see Erik posing in front of them, in the shining light of the Football Dream. And I could see Erik lurking behind me, in the shadows of the clock. (Thursday, October 5)"

5. "Everyone in Tangerine County knows him [Erik] now. Or they think they do. (Thursday, November 2)"

6. "In Lake Windsor Downs, the people were inside, welcoming the freeze with hot cocoa and fake logs and Christmas CDs. In Tangerine, the people were heading out to fight it with shovels and axes and burning tires. (Thursday, November 23)"

7. ""How many games did I play in, Dad?" He pulled back. "I don't know." "What position did I play when I did get into a game?" "How am I supposed to know that?" "OK. Here's one: How many field goals did Erik kick this year?" He stared at me, and then he blinked rapidly. "All right. Your point is taken." (Friday, November 24)"

8. ""We wanted to find a way to keep you from always hating your brother." I answered, "So you figured it would be better if I just hated myself?" (Friday, December 1)"

9. "Don't spend your life hiding under the bleachers, little brother. The truth shall set you free. (Saturday, December 2)"

10. "I started with the basic facts, a paragraph or two, but I couldn't stop there. I had too much to say. I started writing about Luis, and what he meant to the people around him, and how they depended on him, and why they looked up to him. Then I tried to write the same thing about Erik: What did he mean to the people around him? How did they depend on him? Why did they look up to him? I don't suppose the police are interested in all of that. That's not their job. But it's a part of the truth. A big part. And as Antoine Thomas told me, "The truth shall set you free." (Tuesday, December 5, Later)"

V. Vocabulary
    A. Write the vocabulary words you are given. After writing them down, go back and write in their definitions.

Word	Definition
1	
2	
3	
4	
5	
6	
7	
8	
9	
10	

    B. Write a short paragraph using 8 of these 10 words.

Tangerine Advanced Short Answer Unit Test Answer Key

I. Matching

C	1.	FLORIDA	A.	Cause of Luis's death
B	2.	MUCK	B.	This type of fire is continuously burning behind Paul's house.
K	3.	LIGHTNING	C.	State where Paul and his family move at the start of the novel
R	4.	MUD	D.	Paul's nickname at Tangerine
M	5.	KERRI	E.	Antoine's little sister who plays on Paul's soccer team
Q	6.	ARTHUR	F.	How Paul says he would feel if his brother died
H	7.	MARS	G.	The houses tented for ___ were being robbed.
D	8.	FISHER	H.	Paul's nickname at Lake Windsor Downs
J	9.	THERESA	I.	Starts a fight with Joey over a comment he made about Luis
O	10.	GIRLS	J.	Shows Paul around school on the first day
T	11.	JOEY	K.	Kills Mike Castello
L	12.	ANTOINE	L.	Person who pulls the ball away from Erik as he goes to kick for a last minute play
A	13.	ANEURYSM	M.	Girl who likes Paul
N	14.	BLACKJACK	N.	Arthur uses it to hit Luis.
I	15.	TINO	O.	Paul & his mom are shocked to see *they* play on the soccer team.
G	16.	TERMITES	P.	Theresa, Tino, and ___ all work with Paul on a school project.
E	17.	SHANDRA	Q.	Erik's sidekick
P	18.	HENRY	R.	Someone smears this in Paul's face, causing him to start a fight.
S	19.	NULLIFIES	S.	The county ___ all LW victories in which Antoine played.
F	20.	RELIEVED	T.	Transfers to Tangerine Middle School & hates it

Tangerine Multiple Choice Unit Test 1

I. Matching

____ 1. FLORIDA   A. Starts a fight with Joey over a comment he made about Luis

____ 2. MUCK   B. Transfers to Tangerine Middle School & hates it

____ 3. LIGHTNING   C. Shows Paul around school on the first day

____ 4. GOGGLES   D. Erik's sidekick

____ 5. KERRI   E. Antoine's little sister who plays on Paul's soccer team

____ 6. SHOES   F. Theresa, Tino, and ___ all work with Paul on a school project.

____ 7. ARTHUR   G. This type of fire is continuously burning behind Paul's house.

____ 8. HEROES   H. Paul wears these on his eyes while playing soccer.

____ 9. THERESA   I. Paul and Joey act as ___ during the sinkhole disaster.

____ 10. JOEY   J. Kills Mike Castello

____ 11. WAR   K. Former home of the Fisher family

____ 12. ANTOINE   L. State where Paul and his family move at the start of the novel

____ 13. ANEURYSM   M. Tangerine's teams are known as the ___ Eagles.

____ 14. TINO   N. Joey tries to take these off of his brother.

____ 15. SHANDRA   O. Paul helps the Cruz family care for their tangerines during the ___.

____ 16. HENRY   P. Person who pulls the ball away from Erik as he goes to kick for a last minute play

____ 17. FREEZE   Q. Girl who likes Paul

____ 18. HOUSTON   R. Paul occasionally has these, about the past.

____ 19. FLASHBACKS   S. Cause of Luis's death

____ 20. FOOTBALL   T. The Erik Fisher ___ Dream

II. Multiple Choice

1. What does Paul write in his statement for the police?
    A. He tells what happened and then offers ideas for ways Erik could be punished.
    B. He tells what happened, but lies and says that it is more Erik's fault than Arthur's.
    C. He tells what happened and then talks about Luis's life and how he influenced others.
    D. He tells what happened and then describes other bad things Erik has done.

2. What does Paul see while hiding under the bleachers at football practice?
    A. Paul sees Luis come to football practice and shove Erik in the chest for punching his brother. As Luis is talking to his friend, Antoine Thomas, Paul watches as Erik and Arthur break the windshield on Luis's truck and key the paint on the side.
    B. Paul sees Luis come to football practice and push Erik from behind. Luis tells him to never touch his brother again and Erik stands there silent. As Luis walks away, both Arthur and Erik tackle him to the ground and kick him repeatedly.
    C. Paul sees Luis come to football practice looking for Erik. He confronts Erik about punching his brother, and Arthur pulls a blackjack out of his bag and hits Luis in the head. He falls down and is hurt while Erik walks away laughing.
    D. Paul sees Luis come to football practice and talk to Antoine Thomas for a few minutes. The two, who both hate Erik, go up to him and threaten him. Erik shoves them away and Arthur pulls a gun out of his bag, warning them to stay away.

3. Who does Paul think witnessed Erik punching Tino?
    A. Joey
    B. Luis
    C. His dad
    D. His mom

4. What are a few of the unique qualities about the Golden Dawn tangerine?
    A. It is bigger, sweeter, and grows in hot weather.
    B. It is healthier and produces three times the fruit as a normal tangerine.
    C. It is seedless, very juicy, and can withstand cold weather.
    D. It is more colorful and doesn't need soil to grow.

5. Why does Paul's mother call the *Tangerine Times*?
   A. She wants the newspaper to do a feature on the girl soccer players at Tangerine.
   B. She wants the newspaper to do a story on all the kids that transferred to Tangerine.
   C. She wants the newspaper to investigate the poor conditions at Tangerine.
   D. She wants the newspaper to do a story about the kids of the tangerine workers.

6. Why is the whole town laughing at Erik after the first football game?
   A. Erik starts to cry on the sidelines when he learns that Antoine will be holding the ball for his kicks. He has been practicing with Arthur and feels more confident with him holding the ball. Other players see him cry and spread the news around the school and town that Erik cried.
   B. Erik and Antoine are supposed to try a new play to win the game. Erik is usually only a place kicker so he gets confused about what to do. When Antoine gets him the ball, Erik panics and kicks it, but to the other team's end zone.
   C. Erik comes out on the field in his nice clean uniform but doesn't know he has a tear in his pants. As he goes to kick the football his pants split open and the whole crowd can see his underwear.
   D. Erik goes to kick the football and Antoine pulls it away for a two-point conversion. Erik doesn't know what is happening and kicks at nothing, causing him to fly up in the air and land on his back in the mud.

7. A small fight breaks out at soccer practice between Victor and Tino. What is the fight about?
   A. Whether Paul made the save or Victor made the goal
   B. Who should take Shandra's place as goalie
   C. Whether Victor is allowed to date Tino's sister, Theresa
   D. Who should be team captain

8. Why does Paul want to go to Tangerine Middle School so badly?
   A. He can register without an IEP and be eligible to play on the soccer team.
   B. He knows their soccer team is better and wants to be on a winning team.
   C. He wants the chance to start over and make new friends who don't know about his vision problem.
   D. He wants to be as far away from his brother as possible.

9. How does Paul say he would feel if his brother died?
   A. Paul says he would feel happy if his brother died. His feels like his dad never pays attention to him or goes to his soccer games, so if Erik was gone, he would finally get the attention he wants from him dad.
   B. Paul says he would feel devastated if his brother died. Even though they don't really get along, he can't imagine trying to comfort his parents and deal with the emptiness he would feel being the only child.
   C. Paul says he would feel relieved if his brother died. However, he knows that Erik has something to do with the eclipse story and if died that part of the story and what he needs to remember would be gone.
   D. Paul says he would feel excited if his brother died. However, he knows that Erik's death would really hurt his parents and he doesn't want to see them get hurt.

10. What do Paul's grandparents think of "the Erik Fisher Football Dream"?
    A. They hate that Erik plays football. They feel like football isn't safe and constantly tell Erik he should quit.
    B. They couldn't care less about Erik's football career. They change the subject anytime it comes up.
    C. They are just as excited as Paul's parents. They are helping Erik get scholarships to good colleges and hope to see him play in the NFL.
    D. They are equally excited about Erik's football career as they are Paul's soccer career. They are supportive of both grandchildren equally.

11. Why are so many kids absent from school the first day it is cold?
    A. The school doesn't have a heater since it is rarely cold in Florida. Most kids know this and stay home where it is warm.
    B. Most kids are helping their family fight the freeze to keep their fruit and vegetable plants alive.
    C. The kids rarely get a cold weather in Florida. When the first cold front comes many of them skip school to enjoy it.
    D. Most kids have to walk or bike to school. When it is very cold they stay home to avoid the harsh weather.

12. Why is Paul excited about going to St. Anthony's on a trial basis?
    A. He has always been viewed as a nerd but now he has a bad reputation and will be feared.
    B. The school is close to Theresa's house, so he can walk to the groves after school.
    C. The soccer team at St. Anthony's gets private lessons from professional players.
    D. Joey goes to school there, and he will get to spend more time with him.

13. What is Paul's punishment for assaulting a teacher?
    A. He gets suspended for three days.
    B. He gets suspended for three weeks.
    C. He gets sent back to Lake Windsor Middle School.
    D. He gets expelled from all Tangerine public schools.

14. How does Victor try to protect Paul from getting punished for jumping on the coach?
    A. He tells the principal that Paul was just trying to protect them and shouldn't be punished.
    B. He tells the principal that Paul's glasses fell off and he couldn't see what he was doing. He says Paul probably thought he was pulling Victor off the coach.
    C. He tells the principal that Paul fainted or something and fell out of the bleachers and that he wasn't involved at all.
    D. He tells the principal that Paul only helped them because he and Tino threatened to beat him up if he didn't help.

15. What do Paul's grandparents say when they hear about all the trouble Erik is in?
    A. They tell his parents that they should have sent Erik to a doctor when he first hurt Paul, all those years ago.
    B. They are very upset and begin to cry. They blame themselves for not being more involved in his life.
    C. They are shocked and can't believe their grandson could do something like that. They demand to talk to him and get his side of the story.
    D. They tell his parents it was because he played football. They say the sport made him more aggressive and they should have taught him to play something different.

16. What agreement do the Fishers and the Bauers want their neighbors to agree to in regards to their stolen property?
    A. If they only report half of their stolen items, making it a misdemeanor instead of a felony, then the parents will repay each person for all their stolen goods.
    B. If they agree not to sue the families for the stolen property, the parents of each child will make sure each the police prosecute Erik and Arthur to the fullest extent.
    C. If they press charges against the boys they sign an agreement to still let them both play football in college.
    D. If they agree not to press charges and give the boys a second chance, then the families will guarantee the return of all their items or pay for their replacement.

17. Paul confronts his parents about how he lost his eyesight. What excuse do they give him about not telling him the truth?
    A. They didn't want Paul to be afraid of his brother.
    B. They didn't want Paul to tell people this horrible and embarrassing family secret.
    C. They didn't want Erik to go to jail or be forced to see a psychologist.
    D. They didn't want Paul to hate his brother.

18. What does Paul do during Luis's funeral?
    A. He stays at home and finishes the report on the tangerine Luis developed. He adds more to the report in honor of Luis.
    B. He digs a hole underneath the sod and puts his face near it. He remembers Luis and begins to cry. He then buries his tears in the hole.
    C. He stands in the middle of the Golden Dawn tangerine grove all alone. He thinks about Luis and vows to tell the truth about what happened.
    D. He stands just outside of the room where the services are being held. He peers through the door and listens but refuses to go inside near the body.

19. How does Luis die?
    A. Erik and Arthur hear that Luis is going to take revenge on them. They take matters into their own hands and go to the tangerine grove to find Luis. They suffocate him and leave him for dead in the grove.
    B. He suffered from an aneurysm after being hit in the head. A blood clot formed after he was hit by Arthur and it took six days for it to kill him.
    C. He was hit by a frozen tree branch that fell out in the grove. It hit him on the head and knocked him unconscious. No one found him for several hours and by then he had died.
    D. A blood clot forms in the same knee Luis fell on as a child. It prevents blood from flowing to his legs and he becomes paralyzed in the grove. They take him to the hospital, but there is nothing the doctors can do to help his blood flow and he dies.

20. Why does Paul have a hard time believing the story his brother told him about how he damaged his vision?
    A. Paul's brother is known as a big liar.
    B. Paul thinks that if the story is true, he should be able to remember it happening.
    C. Paul's parents laugh at him when he tells the story, making him think it is fake.
    D. Paul finds a hidden newspaper clipping that makes it seem like something suspicious happened.

III. Composition
1. *The Bulletin* said that Tangerine is "a richly imagined read about an underdog coming into his own." Defend that statement using the text for support.

2. Would you say the people and events in *Tangerine* are extraordinary or more universal? Defend your choice with examples from the text.

IV. Vocabulary

____ 1. DISBELIEF   A. Threatening or dangerous

____ 2. CALISTHENICS   B. Refuses to give up or let go; long-lasting

____ 3. ECLIPSE   C. Disliked intensely; scorned; loathed

____ 4. JITTERY   D. Never before known, experienced, or done

____ 5. AFFIDAVITS   E. One's own moral or ethical awareness of right and wrong

____ 6. ELATED   F. Spellbound; enthralled; hypnotized

____ 7. INCONSISTENT   G. Strongly; violently; with forceful expression of emotion or belief

____ 8. BANTER   H. Written statements made under oath

____ 9. MENACING   I. Exercises to develop muscles

____ 10. SCARCE   J. A swell, almost like a bubble, in an artery resulting from the weakening of the blood vessel wall; if it bursts, it is usually fatal

____ 11. CONSCIENCE   K. Extremely tense or nervous

____ 12. TROUNCED   L. The disappearance of the whole or a part of the sun when the moon comes between it and earth, or of the moon when the earth's shadow falls upon it

____ 13. VEHEMENTLY   M. Amazement or astonishment

____ 14. MESMERIZED   N. Twist into a strange shape or expression

____ 15. CONTORT   O. Not regular or predictable

____ 16. DESPISED   P. Light, teasing, playful remarks

____ 17. ANEURYSM   Q. Uncommonly or infrequently found or seen

____ 18. PERSISTENT   R. Violation; breach

____ 19. INFRACTION   S. Beat severely

____ 20. UNPRECEDENTED   T. Very happy or proud; in high spirits

Tangerine Multiple Choice Unit Test 1 Answer Key

I. Matching

L	1.	FLORIDA	A.	Starts a fight with Joey over a comment he made about Luis
G	2.	MUCK	B.	Transfers to Tangerine Middle School & hates it
J	3.	LIGHTNING	C.	Shows Paul around school on the first day
H	4.	GOGGLES	D.	Erik's sidekick
Q	5.	KERRI	E.	Antoine's little sister who plays on Paul's soccer team
N	6.	SHOES	F.	Theresa, Tino, and ___ all work with Paul on a school project.
D	7.	ARTHUR	G.	This type of fire is continuously burning behind Paul's house.
I	8.	HEROES	H.	Paul wears these on his eyes while playing soccer.
C	9.	THERESA	I.	Paul and Joey act as ___ during the sinkhole disaster.
B	10.	JOEY	J.	Kills Mike Castello
M	11.	WAR	K.	Former home of the Fisher family
P	12.	ANTOINE	L.	State where Paul and his family move at the start of the novel
S	13.	ANEURYSM	M.	Tangerine's teams are known as the ___ Eagles.
A	14.	TINO	N.	Joey tries to take these off of his brother.
E	15.	SHANDRA	O.	Paul helps the Cruz family care for their tangerines during the ___.
F	16.	HENRY	P.	Person who pulls the ball away from Erik as he goes to kick for a last minute play
O	17.	FREEZE	Q.	Girl who likes Paul
K	18.	HOUSTON	R.	Paul occasionally has these, about the past.
R	19.	FLASHBACKS	S.	Cause of Luis's death
T	20.	FOOTBALL	T.	The Erik Fisher ___ Dream

II. Multiple Choice

C 1. What does Paul write in his statement for the police?
   A. He tells what happened and then offers ideas for ways Erik could be punished.
   B. He tells what happened, but lies and says that it is more Erik's fault than Arthur's.
   C. He tells what happened and then talks about Luis's life and how he influenced others.
   D. He tells what happened and then describes other bad things Erik has done.

C 2. What does Paul see while hiding under the bleachers at football practice?
   A. Paul sees Luis come to football practice and shove Erik in the chest for punching his brother. As Luis is talking to his friend, Antoine Thomas, Paul watches as Erik and Arthur break the windshield on Luis's truck and key the paint on the side.
   B. Paul sees Luis come to football practice and push Erik from behind. Luis tells him to never touch his brother again and Erik stands there silent. As Luis walks away, both Arthur and Erik tackle him to the ground and kick him repeatedly.
   C. Paul sees Luis come to football practice looking for Erik. He confronts Erik about punching his brother, and Arthur pulls a blackjack out of his bag and hits Luis in the head. He falls down and is hurt while Erik walks away laughing.
   D. Paul sees Luis come to football practice and talk to Antoine Thomas for a few minutes. The two, who both hate Erik, go up to him and threaten him. Erik shoves them away and Arthur pulls a gun out of his bag, warning them to stay away.

C 3. Who does Paul think witnessed Erik punching Tino?
   A. Joey
   B. Luis
   C. His dad
   D. His mom

C 4. What are a few of the unique qualities about the Golden Dawn tangerine?
   A. It is bigger, sweeter, and grows in hot weather.
   B. It is healthier and produces three times the fruit as a normal tangerine.
   C. It is seedless, very juicy, and can withstand cold weather.
   D. It is more colorful and doesn't need soil to grow.

A 5. Why does Paul's mother call the *Tangerine Times*?
- A. She wants the newspaper to do a feature on the girl soccer players at Tangerine.
- B. She wants the newspaper to do a story on all the kids that transferred to Tangerine.
- C. She wants the newspaper to investigate the poor conditions at Tangerine.
- D. She wants the newspaper to do a story about the kids of the tangerine workers.

D 6. Why is the whole town laughing at Erik after the first football game?
- A. Erik starts to cry on the sidelines when he learns that Antoine will be holding the ball for his kicks. He has been practicing with Arthur and feels more confident with him holding the ball. Other players see him cry and spread the news around the school and town that Erik cried.
- B. Erik and Antoine are supposed to try a new play to win the game. Erik is usually only a place kicker so he gets confused about what to do. When Antoine gets him the ball, Erik panics and kicks it, but to the other team's end zone.
- C. Erik comes out on the field in his nice clean uniform but doesn't know he has a tear in his pants. As he goes to kick the football his pants split open and the whole crowd can see his underwear.
- D. Erik goes to kick the football and Antoine pulls it away for a two-point conversion. Erik doesn't know what is happening and kicks at nothing, causing him to fly up in the air and land on his back in the mud.

A 7. A small fight breaks out at soccer practice between Victor and Tino. What is the fight about?
- A. Whether Paul made the save or Victor made the goal
- B. Who should take Shandra's place as goalie
- C. Whether Victor is allowed to date Tino's sister, Theresa
- D. Who should be team captain

A 8. Why does Paul want to go to Tangerine Middle School so badly?
- A. He can register without an IEP and be eligible to play on the soccer team.
- B. He knows their soccer team is better and wants to be on a winning team.
- C. He wants the chance to start over and make new friends who don't know about his vision problem.
- D. He wants to be as far away from his brother as possible.

C 9. How does Paul say he would feel if his brother died?
- A. Paul says he would feel happy if his brother died. His feels like his dad never pays attention to him or goes to his soccer games, so if Erik was gone, he would finally get the attention he wants from him dad.
- B. Paul says he would feel devastated if his brother died. Even though they don't really get along, he can't imagine trying to comfort his parents and deal with the emptiness he would feel being the only child.
- C. Paul says he would feel relieved if his brother died. However, he knows that Erik has something to do with the eclipse story and if died that part of the story and what he needs to remember would be gone.
- D. Paul says he would feel excited if his brother died. However, he knows that Erik's death would really hurt his parents and he doesn't want to see them get hurt.

B 10. What do Paul's grandparents think of "the Erik Fisher Football Dream"?
- A. They hate that Erik plays football. They feel like football isn't safe and constantly tell Erik he should quit.
- B. They couldn't care less about Erik's football career. They change the subject anytime it comes up.
- C. They are just as excited as Paul's parents. They are helping Erik get scholarships to good colleges and hope to see him play in the NFL.
- D. They are equally excited about Erik's football career as they are Paul's soccer career. They are supportive of both grandchildren equally.

B 11. Why are so many kids absent from school the first day it is cold?
- A. The school doesn't have a heater since it is rarely cold in Florida. Most kids know this and stay home where it is warm.
- B. Most kids are helping their family fight the freeze to keep their fruit and vegetable plants alive.
- C. The kids rarely get a cold weather in Florida. When the first cold front comes many of them skip school to enjoy it.
- D. Most kids have to walk or bike to school. When it is very cold they stay home to avoid the harsh weather.

A 12. Why is Paul excited about going to St. Anthony's on a trial basis?
- A. He has always been viewed as a nerd but now he has a bad reputation and will be feared.
- B. The school is close to Theresa's house, so he can walk to the groves after school.
- C. The soccer team at St. Anthony's gets private lessons from professional players.
- D. Joey goes to school there, and he will get to spend more time with him.

D 13. What is Paul's punishment for assaulting a teacher?
- A. He gets suspended for three days.
- B. He gets suspended for three weeks.
- C. He gets sent back to Lake Windsor Middle School.
- D. He gets expelled from all Tangerine public schools.

C 14. How does Victor try to protect Paul from getting punished for jumping on the coach?
- A. He tells the principal that Paul was just trying to protect them and shouldn't be punished.
- B. He tells the principal that Paul's glasses fell off and he couldn't see what he was doing. He says Paul probably thought he was pulling Victor off the coach.
- C. He tells the principal that Paul fainted or something and fell out of the bleachers and that he wasn't involved at all.
- D. He tells the principal that Paul only helped them because he and Tino threatened to beat him up if he didn't help.

A 15. What do Paul's grandparents say when they hear about all the trouble Erik is in?
- A. They tell his parents that they should have sent Erik to a doctor when he first hurt Paul, all those years ago.
- B. They are very upset and begin to cry. They blame themselves for not being more involved in his life.
- C. They are shocked and can't believe their grandson could do something like that. They demand to talk to him and get his side of the story.
- D. They tell his parents it was because he played football. They say the sport made him more aggressive and they should have taught him to play something different.

D 16. What agreement do the Fishers and the Bauers want their neighbors to agree to in regards to their stolen property?
- A. If they only report half of their stolen items, making it a misdemeanor instead of a felony, then the parents will repay each person for all their stolen goods.
- B. If they agree not to sue the families for the stolen property, the parents of each child will make sure each the police prosecute Erik and Arthur to the fullest extent.
- C. If they press charges against the boys they sign an agreement to still let them both play football in college.
- D. If they agree not to press charges and give the boys a second chance, then the families will guarantee the return of all their items or pay for their replacement.

D 17. Paul confronts his parents about how he lost his eyesight. What excuse do they give him about not telling him the truth?
- A. They didn't want Paul to be afraid of his brother.
- B. They didn't want Paul to tell people this horrible and embarrassing family secret.
- C. They didn't want Erik to go to jail or be forced to see a psychologist.
- D. They didn't want Paul to hate his brother.

B 18. What does Paul do during Luis's funeral?
- A. He stays at home and finishes the report on the tangerine Luis developed. He adds more to the report in honor of Luis.
- B. He digs a hole underneath the sod and puts his face near it. He remembers Luis and begins to cry. He then buries his tears in the hole.
- C. He stands in the middle of the Golden Dawn tangerine grove all alone. He thinks about Luis and vows to tell the truth about what happened.
- D. He stands just outside of the room where the services are being held. He peers through the door and listens but refuses to go inside near the body.

B 19. How does Luis die?
- A. Erik and Arthur hear that Luis is going to take revenge on them. They take matters into their own hands and go to the tangerine grove to find Luis. They suffocate him and leave him for dead in the grove.
- B. He suffered from an aneurysm after being hit in the head. A blood clot formed after he was hit by Arthur and it took six days for it to kill him.
- C. He was hit by a frozen tree branch that fell out in the grove. It hit him on the head and knocked him unconscious. No one found him for several hours and by then he had died.
- D. A blood clot forms in the same knee Luis fell on as a child. It prevents blood from flowing to his legs and he becomes paralyzed in the grove. They take him to the hospital, but there is nothing the doctors can do to help his blood flow and he dies.

B 20. Why does Paul have a hard time believing the story his brother told him about how he damaged his vision?
- A. Paul's brother is known as a big liar.
- B. Paul thinks that if the story is true, he should be able to remember it happening.
- C. Paul's parents laugh at him when he tells the story, making him think it is fake.
- D. Paul finds a hidden newspaper clipping that makes it seem like something suspicious happened.

IV. Vocabulary

M	1.	DISBELIEF	A.	Threatening or dangerous
I	2.	CALISTHENICS	B.	Refuses to give up or let go; long-lasting
L	3.	ECLIPSE	C.	Disliked intensely; scorned; loathed
K	4.	JITTERY	D.	Never before known, experienced, or done
H	5.	AFFIDAVITS	E.	One's own moral or ethical awareness of right and wrong
T	6.	ELATED	F.	Spellbound; enthralled; hypnotized
O	7.	INCONSISTENT	G.	Strongly; violently; with forceful expression of emotion or belief
P	8.	BANTER	H.	Written statements made under oath
A	9.	MENACING	I.	Exercises to develop muscles
Q	10.	SCARCE	J.	A swell, almost like a bubble, in an artery resulting from the weakening of the blood vessel wall; if it bursts, it is usually fatal
E	11.	CONSCIENCE	K.	Extremely tense or nervous
S	12.	TROUNCED	L.	The disappearance of the whole or a part of the sun when the moon comes between it and earth, or of the moon when the earth's shadow falls upon it
G	13.	VEHEMENTLY	M.	Amazement or astonishment
F	14.	MESMERIZED	N.	Twist into a strange shape or expression
N	15.	CONTORT	O.	Not regular or predictable
C	16.	DESPISED	P.	Light, teasing, playful remarks
J	17.	ANEURYSM	Q.	Uncommonly or infrequently found or seen
B	18.	PERSISTENT	R.	Violation; breach
R	19.	INFRACTION	S.	Beat severely
D	20.	UNPRECEDENTED	T.	Very happy or proud; in high spirits

Tangerine Multiple Choice Unit Test 2

I. Matching

____ 1.	MUCK	A.	Paul's nickname at Lake Windsor Downs
____ 2.	LIGHTNING	B.	Starts a fight with Joey over a comment he made about Luis
____ 3.	GOGGLES	C.	Position on the soccer team Paul has always played in the past
____ 4.	GOALIE	D.	Paul wears these on his eyes while playing soccer.
____ 5.	KERRI	E.	Paul's nickname at Tangerine
____ 6.	SHOES	F.	Paul & his mom are shocked to see *they* play on the soccer team.
____ 7.	MARS	G.	This type of fire is continuously burning behind Paul's house.
____ 8.	FISHER	H.	Transfers to Tangerine Middle School & hates it
____ 9.	IEP	I.	Shows Paul around school on the first day
____ 10.	HEROES	J.	Tino and Victor go to the ___ ceremony to get revenge on Erik.
____ 11.	THERESA	K.	Joey tries to take these off of his brother.
____ 12.	GIRLS	L.	Kills Mike Castello
____ 13.	JOEY	M.	Prevents Paul from playing soccer at LWD; later "disappears"
____ 14.	WAR	N.	Paul's mom finds the stolen goods in the ___ unit.
____ 15.	ANEURYSM	O.	Cause of Luis's death
____ 16.	BLACKJACK	P.	Tangerine's teams are known as the ___ Eagles.
____ 17.	TINO	Q.	Paul and Joey act as ___ during the sinkhole disaster.
____ 18.	STORAGE	R.	Arthur uses it to hit Luis.
____ 19.	AWARD	S.	Former home of the Fisher family
____ 20.	HOUSTON	T.	Girl who likes Paul

II. Multiple Choice

1. Why does Paul have a hard time believing the story his brother told him about how he damaged his vision?
    A. Paul finds a hidden newspaper clipping that makes it seem like something suspicious happened.
    B. Paul thinks that if the story is true, he should be able to remember it happening.
    C. Paul's brother is known as a big liar.
    D. Paul's parents laugh at him when he tells the story, making him think it is fake.

2. What does Paul see while hiding under the bleachers at football practice?
    A. Paul sees Luis come to football practice and push Erik from behind. Luis tells him to never touch his brother again and Erik stands there silent. As Luis walks away, both Arthur and Erik tackle him to the ground and kick him repeatedly.
    B. Paul sees Luis come to football practice and talk to Antoine Thomas for a few minutes. The two, who both hate Erik, go up to him and threaten him. Erik shoves them away and Arthur pulls a gun out of his bag, warning them to stay away.
    C. Paul sees Luis come to football practice looking for Erik. He confronts Erik about punching his brother, and Arthur pulls a blackjack out of his bag and hits Luis in the head. He falls down and is hurt while Erik walks away laughing.
    D. Paul sees Luis come to football practice and shove Erik in the chest for punching his brother. As Luis is talking to his friend, Antoine Thomas, Paul watches as Erik and Arthur break the windshield on Luis's truck and key the paint on the side.

3. Why did the Golden Dawn tangerines survive so easily?
    A. They are designed to survive in heavy snow.
    B. They are all in portable pots and could be moved inside the house.
    C. They are all small and could be saved by covering them with dirt.
    D. They are all small and could be saved by covering them with blankets.

4. How does Luis die?
    A. He suffered from an aneurysm after being hit in the head. A blood clot formed after he was hit by Arthur and it took six days for it to kill him.
    B. A blood clot forms in the same knee Luis fell on as a child. It prevents blood from flowing to his legs and he becomes paralyzed in the grove. They take him to the hospital, but there is nothing the doctors can do to help his blood flow and he dies.
    C. He was hit by a frozen tree branch that fell out in the grove. It hit him on the head and knocked him unconscious. No one found him for several hours and by then he had died.
    D. Erik and Arthur hear that Luis is going to take revenge on them. They take matters into their own hands and go to the tangerine grove to find Luis. They suffocate him and leave him for dead in the grove.

5. What does Paul do during Luis's funeral?
    A. He digs a hole underneath the sod and puts his face near it. He remembers Luis and begins to cry. He then buries his tears in the hole.
    B. He stays at home and finishes the report on the tangerine Luis developed. He adds more to the report in honor of Luis.
    C. He stands in the middle of the Golden Dawn tangerine grove all alone. He thinks about Luis and vows to tell the truth about what happened.
    D. He stands just outside of the room where the services are being held. He peers through the door and listens but refuses to go inside near the body.

6. Paul confronts his parents about how he lost his eyesight. What excuse do they give him about not telling him the truth?
    A. They didn't want Paul to hate his brother.
    B. They didn't want Paul to be afraid of his brother.
    C. They didn't want Erik to go to jail or be forced to see a psychologist.
    D. They didn't want Paul to tell people this horrible and embarrassing family secret.

7. What strategy does Paul's dad want to use in fighting the football scandal?
    A. He wants to have the newspaper recognize all the accomplishments of the other players to prove that Antoine wasn't the one creating all the team victories.
    B. He wants to sue Antoine and his family for lying and damaging the records and statistics of the other players.
    C. He wants to lie and say he knew nothing about Antoine's living situation so he can place all the blame on Antoine and pretend no one else knew anything about what was really happening.
    D. He wants to contact all the colleges to formally announce that no one else on the team had anything to do with the scandal so colleges will still recruit other players.

8. What is Paul's punishment for assaulting a teacher?
    A. He gets suspended for three weeks.
    B. He gets expelled from all Tangerine public schools.
    C. He gets sent back to Lake Windsor Middle School.
    D. He gets suspended for three days.

9. Why is Paul excited about going to St. Anthony's on a trial basis?
    A. He has always been viewed as a nerd but now he has a bad reputation and will be feared.
    B. Joey goes to school there, and he will get to spend more time with him.
    C. The school is close to Theresa's house, so he can walk to the groves after school.
    D. The soccer team at St. Anthony's gets private lessons from professional players.

10. Why is the soccer game against Lake Windsor Middle School such a big deal?
    A. The winning team wins a trip to Washington, DC to play in the national championship.
    B. The winning team goes to the state competition at the University of Florida.
    C. The winning team get a huge trophy to display in their school.
    D. The winning team will be the county champion since both teams are undefeated.

11. Why did Luis have to play goalie in soccer?
    A. He got in too many fights when he was out on the field with other players.
    B. He was handicapped and couldn't move around the field.
    C. He had asthma and had trouble breathing if he ran too much.
    D. He was the only one who had played goalie before.

12. How does Arthur benefit from Mike's death?
    A. He is the new boyfriend of Mike's popular girlfriend.
    B. He is the one who gets to hold the ball for Erik's kicks.
    C. He is the new quarterback for the team.
    D. He is the new valedictorian.

13. Why is Paul kicked off the soccer team?
    A. He gets angry at another player for making fun of him and starts a fight. Both boys get kicked off the team for misconduct.
    B. His grades are too low to be eligible to participate in after-school sports.
    C. He is labeled as handicapped because of his vision and isn't covered by the school insurance.
    D. He isn't as good as the eighth grade goalie, so they tell him he is cut from the team unless he wants to be the water boy.

14. What do Paul and Joey do when they see the portables being swallowed up by the sinkhole?
    A. Help rescue people trapped in the portables
    B. Videotape the scene to later be played on CNN
    C. Run with other kids to the high school for safety
    D. Call 911 to get help

15. Why does Paul want to go to Tangerine Middle School so badly?
    A. He wants the chance to start over and make new friends who don't know about his vision problem.
    B. He can register without an IEP and be eligible to play on the soccer team.
    C. He wants to be as far away from his brother as possible.
    D. He knows their soccer team is better and wants to be on a winning team.

16. What happens when Paul goes in for Victor in the team's first home game?
    A. He gets knocked over by a bigger player.
    B. He can't find his goggles and he has to play blind.
    C. He scores the first goal of his life.
    D. He misses a penalty kick that would have won the game for his team.

17. What are a few of the unique qualities about the Golden Dawn tangerine?
    A. It is seedless, very juicy, and can withstand cold weather.
    B. It is more colorful and doesn't need soil to grow.
    C. It is healthier and produces three times the fruit as a normal tangerine.
    D. It is bigger, sweeter, and grows in hot weather.

18. In trying to get rid of the muck fires, what new problem did Paul's neighborhood create?
    A. Mosquitos
    B. Bugs
    C. Flooding
    D. Smoke

19. What interesting file does Paul find on his dad's computer?
    A. Paul--Vision Story
    B. Truth--Paul
    C. Court Dates--Erik
    D. Erik--Scholarship Offers

20. What does Paul write in his statement for the police?
    A. He tells what happened, but lies and says that it is more Erik's fault than Arthur's.
    B. He tells what happened and then describes other bad things Erik has done.
    C. He tells what happened and then talks about Luis's life and how he influenced others.
    D. He tells what happened and then offers ideas for ways Erik could be punished.

III. Composition
1. Choose four events in the book and explain how each one helped Paul grow a little more.

2. Who was responsible for Luis's death? Defend your answer using specific information from the text.

IV. Vocabulary

____ 1. VICIOUS   A. Focus one's attention on (usually a thought) for an extended time
____ 2. ABRUPTLY   B. Strong, vindictive, or fierce anger
____ 3. PERIMETER   C. One leg on either side of; straddling
____ 4. SINGED   D. In a way that is boldly rude or disrespectful
____ 5. DWELL   E. Filled with distress, suffering, or torture; worrying in a distressed way
____ 6. HEAVE   F. Ferocious; unpleasantly severe
____ 7. ELATED   G. Legally obligated or responsible
____ 8. DISINFECTANT   H. Chemical agent used to destroy bacteria
____ 9. MENACING   I. Burned slightly; scorched
____ 10. DECOY   J. Was in deep thought; focused attention on a subject persistently
____ 11. SCARCE   K. Having folds, ridges, and grooves
____ 12. LIABLE   L. Threatening or dangerous
____ 13. INSOLENTLY   M. Twist into a strange shape or expression
____ 14. CONTORT   N. Something or someone used to lure or mislead another into a trap
____ 15. AGONIZING   O. Uncommonly or infrequently found or seen
____ 16. CORRUGATED   P. Suddenly or unexpectedly
____ 17. BROODED   Q. Very happy or proud; in high spirits
____ 18. ASTRIDE   R. Rise up or swell; bulge; lift
____ 19. WRATH   S. Required; bonded
____ 20. OBLIGED   T. Border or boundary

Tangerine Multiple Choice Unit Test 2 Answer Key

I. Matching

G	1.	MUCK	A.	Paul's nickname at Lake Windsor Downs
L	2.	LIGHTNING	B.	Starts a fight with Joey over a comment he made about Luis
D	3.	GOGGLES	C.	Position on the soccer team Paul has always played in the past
C	4.	GOALIE	D.	Paul wears these on his eyes while playing soccer.
T	5.	KERRI	E.	Paul's nickname at Tangerine
K	6.	SHOES	F.	Paul & his mom are shocked to see *they* play on the soccer team.
A	7.	MARS	G.	This type of fire is continuously burning behind Paul's house.
E	8.	FISHER	H.	Transfers to Tangerine Middle School & hates it
M	9.	IEP	I.	Shows Paul around school on the first day
Q	10.	HEROES	J.	Tino and Victor go to the ___ ceremony to get revenge on Erik.
I	11.	THERESA	K.	Joey tries to take these off of his brother.
F	12.	GIRLS	L.	Kills Mike Castello
H	13.	JOEY	M.	Prevents Paul from playing soccer at LWD; later "disappears"
P	14.	WAR	N.	Paul's mom finds the stolen goods in the ___ unit.
O	15.	ANEURYSM	O.	Cause of Luis's death
R	16.	BLACKJACK	P.	Tangerine's teams are known as the ___ Eagles.
B	17.	TINO	Q.	Paul and Joey act as ___ during the sinkhole disaster.
N	18.	STORAGE	R.	Arthur uses it to hit Luis.
J	19.	AWARD	S.	Former home of the Fisher family
S	20.	HOUSTON	T.	Girl who likes Paul

II. Multiple Choice

B 1. Why does Paul have a hard time believing the story his brother told him about how he damaged his vision?
- A. Paul finds a hidden newspaper clipping that makes it seem like something suspicious happened.
- B. Paul thinks that if the story is true, he should be able to remember it happening.
- C. Paul's brother is known as a big liar.
- D. Paul's parents laugh at him when he tells the story, making him think it is fake.

C 2. What does Paul see while hiding under the bleachers at football practice?
- A. Paul sees Luis come to football practice and push Erik from behind. Luis tells him to never touch his brother again and Erik stands there silent. As Luis walks away, both Arthur and Erik tackle him to the ground and kick him repeatedly.
- B. Paul sees Luis come to football practice and talk to Antoine Thomas for a few minutes. The two, who both hate Erik, go up to him and threaten him. Erik shoves them away and Arthur pulls a gun out of his bag, warning them to stay away.
- C. Paul sees Luis come to football practice looking for Erik. He confronts Erik about punching his brother, and Arthur pulls a blackjack out of his bag and hits Luis in the head. He falls down and is hurt while Erik walks away laughing.
- D. Paul sees Luis come to football practice and shove Erik in the chest for punching his brother. As Luis is talking to his friend, Antoine Thomas, Paul watches as Erik and Arthur break the windshield on Luis's truck and key the paint on the side.

C 3. Why did the Golden Dawn tangerines survive so easily?
- A. They are designed to survive in heavy snow.
- B. They are all in portable pots and could be moved inside the house.
- C. They are all small and could be saved by covering them with dirt.
- D. They are all small and could be saved by covering them with blankets.

A 4. How does Luis die?
- A. He suffered from an aneurysm after being hit in the head. A blood clot formed after he was hit by Arthur and it took six days for it to kill him.
- B. A blood clot forms in the same knee Luis fell on as a child. It prevents blood from flowing to his legs and he becomes paralyzed in the grove. They take him to the hospital, but there is nothing the doctors can do to help his blood flow and he dies.
- C. He was hit by a frozen tree branch that fell out in the grove. It hit him on the head and knocked him unconscious. No one found him for several hours and by then he had died.
- D. Erik and Arthur hear that Luis is going to take revenge on them. They take matters into their own hands and go to the tangerine grove to find Luis. They suffocate him and leave him for dead in the grove.

A 5. What does Paul do during Luis's funeral?
- A. He digs a hole underneath the sod and puts his face near it. He remembers Luis and begins to cry. He then buries his tears in the hole.
- B. He stays at home and finishes the report on the tangerine Luis developed. He adds more to the report in honor of Luis.
- C. He stands in the middle of the Golden Dawn tangerine grove all alone. He thinks about Luis and vows to tell the truth about what happened.
- D. He stands just outside of the room where the services are being held. He peers through the door and listens but refuses to go inside near the body.

A 6. Paul confronts his parents about how he lost his eyesight. What excuse do they give him about not telling him the truth?
- A. They didn't want Paul to hate his brother.
- B. They didn't want Paul to be afraid of his brother.
- C. They didn't want Erik to go to jail or be forced to see a psychologist.
- D. They didn't want Paul to tell people this horrible and embarrassing family secret.

C 7. What strategy does Paul's dad want to use in fighting the football scandal?
- A. He wants to have the newspaper recognize all the accomplishments of the other players to prove that Antoine wasn't the one creating all the team victories.
- B. He wants to sue Antoine and his family for lying and damaging the records and statistics of the other players.
- C. He wants to lie and say he knew nothing about Antoine's living situation so he can place all the blame on Antoine and pretend no one else knew anything about what was really happening.
- D. He wants to contact all the colleges to formally announce that no one else on the team had anything to do with the scandal so colleges will still recruit other players.

B 8. What is Paul's punishment for assaulting a teacher?
- A. He gets suspended for three weeks.
- B. He gets expelled from all Tangerine public schools.
- C. He gets sent back to Lake Windsor Middle School.
- D. He gets suspended for three days.

A 9. Why is Paul excited about going to St. Anthony's on a trial basis?
   A. He has always been viewed as a nerd but now he has a bad reputation and will be feared.
   B. Joey goes to school there, and he will get to spend more time with him.
   C. The school is close to Theresa's house, so he can walk to the groves after school.
   D. The soccer team at St. Anthony's gets private lessons from professional players.

D 10. Why is the soccer game against Lake Windsor Middle School such a big deal?
   A. The winning team wins a trip to Washington, DC to play in the national championship.
   B. The winning team goes to the state competition at the University of Florida.
   C. The winning team get a huge trophy to display in their school.
   D. The winning team will be the county champion since both teams are undefeated.

B 11. Why did Luis have to play goalie in soccer?
   A. He got in too many fights when he was out on the field with other players.
   B. He was handicapped and couldn't move around the field.
   C. He had asthma and had trouble breathing if he ran too much.
   D. He was the only one who had played goalie before.

B 12. How does Arthur benefit from Mike's death?
   A. He is the new boyfriend of Mike's popular girlfriend.
   B. He is the one who gets to hold the ball for Erik's kicks.
   C. He is the new quarterback for the team.
   D. He is the new valedictorian.

C 13. Why is Paul kicked off the soccer team?
- A. He gets angry at another player for making fun of him and starts a fight. Both boys get kicked off the team for misconduct.
- B. His grades are too low to be eligible to participate in after-school sports.
- C. He is labeled as handicapped because of his vision and isn't covered by the school insurance.
- D. He isn't as good as the eighth grade goalie, so they tell him he is cut from the team unless he wants to be the water boy.

A 14. What do Paul and Joey do when they see the portables being swallowed up by the sinkhole?
- A. Help rescue people trapped in the portables
- B. Videotape the scene to later be played on CNN
- C. Run with other kids to the high school for safety
- D. Call 911 to get help

B 15. Why does Paul want to go to Tangerine Middle School so badly?
- A. He wants the chance to start over and make new friends who don't know about his vision problem.
- B. He can register without an IEP and be eligible to play on the soccer team.
- C. He wants to be as far away from his brother as possible.
- D. He knows their soccer team is better and wants to be on a winning team.

C 16. What happens when Paul goes in for Victor in the team's first home game?
- A. He gets knocked over by a bigger player.
- B. He can't find his goggles and he has to play blind.
- C. He scores the first goal of his life.
- D. He misses a penalty kick that would have won the game for his team.

A 17. What are a few of the unique qualities about the Golden Dawn tangerine?
- A. It is seedless, very juicy, and can withstand cold weather.
- B. It is more colorful and doesn't need soil to grow.
- C. It is healthier and produces three times the fruit as a normal tangerine.
- D. It is bigger, sweeter, and grows in hot weather.

A 18. In trying to get rid of the muck fires, what new problem did Paul's neighborhood create?
- A. Mosquitos
- B. Bugs
- C. Flooding
- D. Smoke

D 19. What interesting file does Paul find on his dad's computer?
- A. Paul--Vision Story
- B. Truth--Paul
- C. Court Dates--Erik
- D. Erik--Scholarship Offers

C 20. What does Paul write in his statement for the police?
- A. He tells what happened, but lies and says that it is more Erik's fault than Arthur's.
- B. He tells what happened and then describes other bad things Erik has done.
- C. He tells what happened and then talks about Luis's life and how he influenced others.
- D. He tells what happened and then offers ideas for ways Erik could be punished.

IV. Vocabulary

F	1.	VICIOUS	A.	Focus one's attention on (usually a thought) for an extended time
P	2.	ABRUPTLY	B.	Strong, vindictive, or fierce anger
T	3.	PERIMETER	C.	One leg on either side of; straddling
I	4.	SINGED	D.	In a way that is boldly rude or disrespectful
A	5.	DWELL	E.	Filled with distress, suffering, or torture; worrying in a distressed way
R	6.	HEAVE	F.	Ferocious; unpleasantly severe
Q	7.	ELATED	G.	Legally obligated or responsible
H	8.	DISINFECTANT	H.	Chemical agent used to destroy bacteria
L	9.	MENACING	I.	Burned slightly; scorched
N	10.	DECOY	J.	Was in deep thought; focused attention on a subject persistently
O	11.	SCARCE	K.	Having folds, ridges, and grooves
G	12.	LIABLE	L.	Threatening or dangerous
D	13.	INSOLENTLY	M.	Twist into a strange shape or expression
M	14.	CONTORT	N.	Something or someone used to lure or mislead another into a trap
E	15.	AGONIZING	O.	Uncommonly or infrequently found or seen
K	16.	CORRUGATED	P.	Suddenly or unexpectedly
J	17.	BROODED	Q.	Very happy or proud; in high spirits
C	18.	ASTRIDE	R.	Rise up or swell; bulge; lift
B	19.	WRATH	S.	Required; bonded
S	20.	OBLIGED	T.	Border or boundary

UNIT RESOURCE MATERIALS

BULLETIN BOARD IDEAS *Tangerine*

1. Save one corner of the board for the best of students' *Tangerine* writing assignments.
2. Take one of the word search puzzles from the extra activities packet and with a marker copy it over in a large size on the bulletin board. Write the clue words to find to one side. Invite students prior to and after class to find the words and circle them on the bulletin board.
3. Write several of the most significant quotations from the book onto the board on brightly colored paper.
4. Make a bulletin board listing the vocabulary words for this unit. As you complete sections of the novel and discuss the vocabulary for each section, write the definitions on the bulletin board. (If your board is one students face frequently, it will help them learn the words.)
5. Post photos and information about athletes with disabilities. You might also want to post articles from magazines featuring these athletes on your bulletin board as well.
6. Create a bulletin board revolving around the Florida environment. Be sure to include information about lightning, muck fires, sink holes, mosquitoes, and wildlife, along with a map of the state.
7. Create a bulletin board with information about the tangerine/citrus industry. Include information about creating new varieties and damaging weather conditions.
8. Make a bulletin board featuring other teen novels about sports. Write a short tease for each novel and include colorful photos of the book covers to generate interest.

RELATED TOPICS *Tangerine*

1. Disabled Athletes
2. Soccer
3. Football
4. Aids For People Who Are Blind
5. Coping With the Death of a Classmate
6. Lightning
7. Revenge
8. Great Team Rivalries
9. High School Sports
10. Environmental Concerns in Florida
11. Sibling Rivalry
12. Citrus Industry
13. Heroes
14. Traumatic Events
15. Moving to a Different Town

MORE ACTIVITIES *Tangerine*

1. Have students design a new book cover (front and back and inside flaps) for *Tangerine*.
2. Have students design a bulletin board (ready to be put up; not just sketched) for *Tangerine*.
3. Have students group the chapters together to show the larger structure of the novel. Have them explain why they chose the divisions they made.
4. Have students choose one chapter of the book (with sufficient action) to rewrite as a play. In conjunction with this assignment, have students write a composition explaining the difficulties they encountered in changing from one written form to another.
5. Have students write out the characters in the book and cast famous actors and actresses for a movie version of the novel. Instruct students to write a brief explanation as to why the actor/actress they selected would be perfect for the part.
6. Have students create a soundtrack for *Tangerine*. Have students burn a cd of the songs, design a cd cover, and include a brief explanation as to why they selected each song.
7. Have students write a mystery story of their own with a cover page and illustrations.
8. Have students do research on an athlete with a disability. Tell them to then create a poster with pictures and information about the athlete.
9. Have students write a continuation to the story. Instruct them to pick up the novel a few months after the ending date and give information on what is happening with each character.
10. Paul acts as a hero when he is saving kids from the portable during the sinkhole disaster. Have students research other ordinary people who have done something heroic.
11. The sinkhole disaster takes place on September 11. Have students compare and contrast the disaster Paul experiences with the disaster America experienced on this same date.
12. Throughout the story the author reinforces the struggle between nature and man. Have students come up with their own examples of struggles between man and nature throughout the world.
13. Have students read excerpts from How Soccer Explains the World: An Unlikely Theory of Globalization by Franklin Foer.
14. Have students write a letter to the author (see the following handout). Letters can be emailed to: ebloor@edwardbloor.net
15. Have students select a character from the book and complete the "I Am" poem from that character's point of view. (see the following handout)

Letter to the Author

Often times, books are written to make people think about serious issues. Think about the point the author was trying to make in putting together this story. Then, compose a letter to the author expressing how this book has affected your life.

Topics to include in your letter:
- What you liked about the book
- How you could relate to this book
- How realistic the book was
- What you learned from the book
- What issues the book made you think about
- How you felt when reading the book
- How you have changed since reading the book
- Anything else you think the author should know

Necessary Elements:
- Your letter must by typed
- You should begin your letter by saying Dear Mr. (or Ms.) _____,
- You should have an introductory paragraph where you introduce yourself
- You should have body paragraphs
- You should have a friendly conclusion to the letter
- Underneath your signature you should include your home address and email address in case the editor wishes to write you back

Remember to proofread this letter and turn it in to me free of errors. I will grade your letter, allow you to make any changes that are needed, and then I will mail your letters to the author of the book. Most authors enjoy receiving letters from readers and like to see how their hard work has affected others. Some may even respond to letters from their readers, so don't be surprised if you get a reply.

"I Am" Poem

Complete this "I am" poem. You may select any character from the book to do this poem about. Be sure to write from his or her point of view and think about the things he or she would feel. You may use some short one word answers, but do not make each line only a few words. You should try to provide support from the novel to really develop this poem so that it reveals information and insight about the character you select.

I am (2 characteristics your character has)
I wonder (something your character wonders)
I hear (something real or imaginary your character hears)
I see (something real or imaginary your character sees)
I want (something your character desires)
I am (the first line of the poem repeated)

I pretend (something your character pretends to do)
I feel (something real or imaginary your character feels emotionally)
I touch (something real or imaginary your character would touch physically)
I worry (something your characters worries about)
I cry (something that makes your character upset)
I am (the first line of the poem repeated)

I understand (something your character knows)
I say (something your character believes in)
I dream (something your character would dream about)
I try (something your character makes an effort to do)
I hope (something your character hopes for)
I am (the first line of the poem repeated)

UNIT WORD LIST *Tangerine*

No.	Word	Clue/Definition
1.	ANEURYSM	Cause of Luis's death
2.	ANTOINE	Person who pulls the ball away from Erik as he goes to kick for a last minute play
3.	ARTHUR	Erik's sidekick
4.	AWARD	Tino and Victor go to the ___ ceremony to get revenge on Erik.
5.	BLACKJACK	Arthur uses it to hit Luis.
6.	BRIGHT	Coach who participated in the Olympics for track and field
7.	BROTHER	Tino calls Paul this, letting him know everything is good in their friendship
8.	BUS	Being on the ___ at Lake Windsor means you get to play the away games.
9.	CARNIVAL	Paul rats out the Tangerine soccer players for vandalizing an exhibit at the ___.
10.	DAWN	Luis creates a tangerine called the Golden ___.
11.	ECLIPSE	Paul tells people he looked at an ___ for too long, causing damage to his eyes
12.	EXPELLED	Paul gets ___ from school for his actions at the award ceremony.
13.	FISHER	Paul's nickname at Tangerine
14.	FLASHBACKS	Paul occasionally has these, about the past.
15.	FLORIDA	State where Paul and his family move at the start of the novel
16.	FOOTBALL	The Erik Fisher ___ Dream
17.	FREEZE	Paul helps the Cruz family care for their tangerines during the ___.
18.	FUNERAL	Paul is asked not to attend Luis's.
19.	GIRLS	Paul & his mom are shocked to see *they* play on the soccer team.
20.	GOALIE	Position on the soccer team Paul has always played in the past
21.	GOGGLES	Paul wears these on his eyes while playing soccer.
22.	GRANDPARENTS	Paul's are not interested in the Erik Fisher Football Dream.
23.	HENRY	Theresa, Tino, and ___ all work with Paul on a school project.
24.	HEROES	Paul and Joey act as ___ during the sinkhole disaster.
25.	HOUSTON	Former home of the Fisher family
26.	IEP	Prevents Paul from playing soccer at LWD; later "disappears"
27.	JOEY	Transfers to Tangerine Middle School & hates it
28.	KERRI	Girl who likes Paul
29.	LIGHTNING	Kills Mike Castello
30.	MARS	Paul's nickname at Lake Windsor Downs
31.	MORNING	Paul's mom wants practice moved to this time of day.
32.	MOSQUITOES	Side effect of soaking the fields in water to get rid of the fires
33.	MUCK	This type of fire is continuously burning behind Paul's house.
34.	MUD	Someone smears this in Paul's face, causing him to start a fight.

No.	Word	Clue/Definition
35.	NULLIFIES	The county ___ all LW victories in which Antoine played.
36.	OSPREYS	Cause the coy in the pond to disappear
37.	PAUL	His older brother gets all the attention of his parents.
38.	POLICE	Paul prepares a statement for the ___ explaining what he witnessed.
39.	PUNCH	Paul thinks his dad saw Erik ___ Tino but did nothing.
40.	RELIEVED	How Paul says he would feel if his brother died
41.	SCHOLARSHIP	Paul finds a file on his dad's computer about Erik's ___ offers.
42.	SHANDRA	Antoine's little sister who plays on Paul's soccer team
43.	SHOES	Joey tries to take these off of his brother.
44.	SINKHOLE	Does severe damage to Lake Windsor Middle School
45.	SOCCER	Paul's sport
46.	STORAGE	Paul's mom finds the stolen goods in the ___ unit.
47.	TERMITES	The houses tented for ___ were being robbed.
48.	THERESA	Shows Paul around school on the first day
49.	THREE	Number of times lightning has struck Mr. Donnelly's house
50.	TINO	Starts a fight with Joey over a comment he made about Luis
51.	TREE	Luis hurts his leg permanently from falling out of one.
52.	WAR	Tangerine's teams are known as the ___ Eagles.

WORD SEARCH - Tangerine

```
H T H E R E S A S O C C E R B R I G H T P R H
E Q J F U F E S T K S D A M E B V N P I V E C
N G L U H R T M N H M X Y R E X M Y H L X L W
R H Z N T D I S E Q W P X I N S P S W S B I L
Y R B E R M M B R B W W L G Y I R E A L Y E L
N J T R A R R J A Z B A F R T A V R L C S V S
M Z Y A S O E F P K O V U Q L S D A B L V E D
Z O T L T K T G D G M E Q O Q N E W L S E D K
Z Y S H P Z E L N J N H H A N T F V T B D T
X V E Q Y Z G R A A F C G H I T S Q V P J G N
J R J T U R C R R F S J S O B G X R D W B N R
Z X X P B I M E G I K T T W F N D C Q T L V V
S G L F R J T L T Q C N D V J I W C F L A M H
L T O N T N Q O V E A N W Z L N E Z D J C O H
K W O G W T D H S S C F F B S T Z W V V K R G
Y G J R G B B K T P H O G R Z H E W N S J N H
Q L S B A L X N Y I C O B E R G E Z E D A I R
V L Z S C G E I R L H T U H F I R I U Z C N D
H E R O E S E S K C A B H S A L F M U C K G V
J T Q M D C P L N E W A J I T I O V A Q X T J
O B B Y I M U U X Q A L Y F L O N R S R E I W
E B U L K A P M D W R L Q L S W N P I E S N G
Y S O S P R E Y S Z D B U W A R E N R D G O R
Y P G I R L S H O E S N G D C I K T M B A L Z
```

ANEURYSM	FUNERAL	NULLIFIES
ANTOINE	GIRLS	OSPREYS
ARTHUR	GOALIE	PAUL
AWARD	GOGGLES	POLICE
BLACKJACK	GRANDPARENTS	PUNCH
BRIGHT	HENRY	RELIEVED
BROTHER	HEROES	SCHOLARSHIP
BUS	HOUSTON	SHANDRA
CARNIVAL	IEP	SHOES
DAWN	JOEY	SINKHOLE
ECLIPSE	KERRI	SOCCER
EXPELLED	LIGHTNING	STORAGE
FISHER	MARS	TERMITES
FLASHBACKS	MORNING	THERESA
FLORIDA	MOSQUITOS	TINO
FOOTBALL	MUCK	TREE
FREEZE	MUD	WAR

ANSWER KEY WORD SEARCH - Tangerine

ANEURYSM	FUNERAL	NULLIFIES
ANTOINE	GIRLS	OSPREYS
ARTHUR	GOALIE	PAUL
AWARD	GOGGLES	POLICE
BLACKJACK	GRANDPARENTS	PUNCH
BRIGHT	HENRY	RELIEVED
BROTHER	HEROES	SCHOLARSHIP
BUS	HOUSTON	SHANDRA
CARNIVAL	IEP	SHOES
DAWN	JOEY	SINKHOLE
ECLIPSE	KERRI	SOCCER
EXPELLED	LIGHTNING	STORAGE
FISHER	MARS	TERMITES
FLASHBACKS	MORNING	THERESA
FLORIDA	MOSQUITOS	TINO
FOOTBALL	MUCK	TREE
FREEZE	MUD	WAR

CROSSWORD - Tangerine

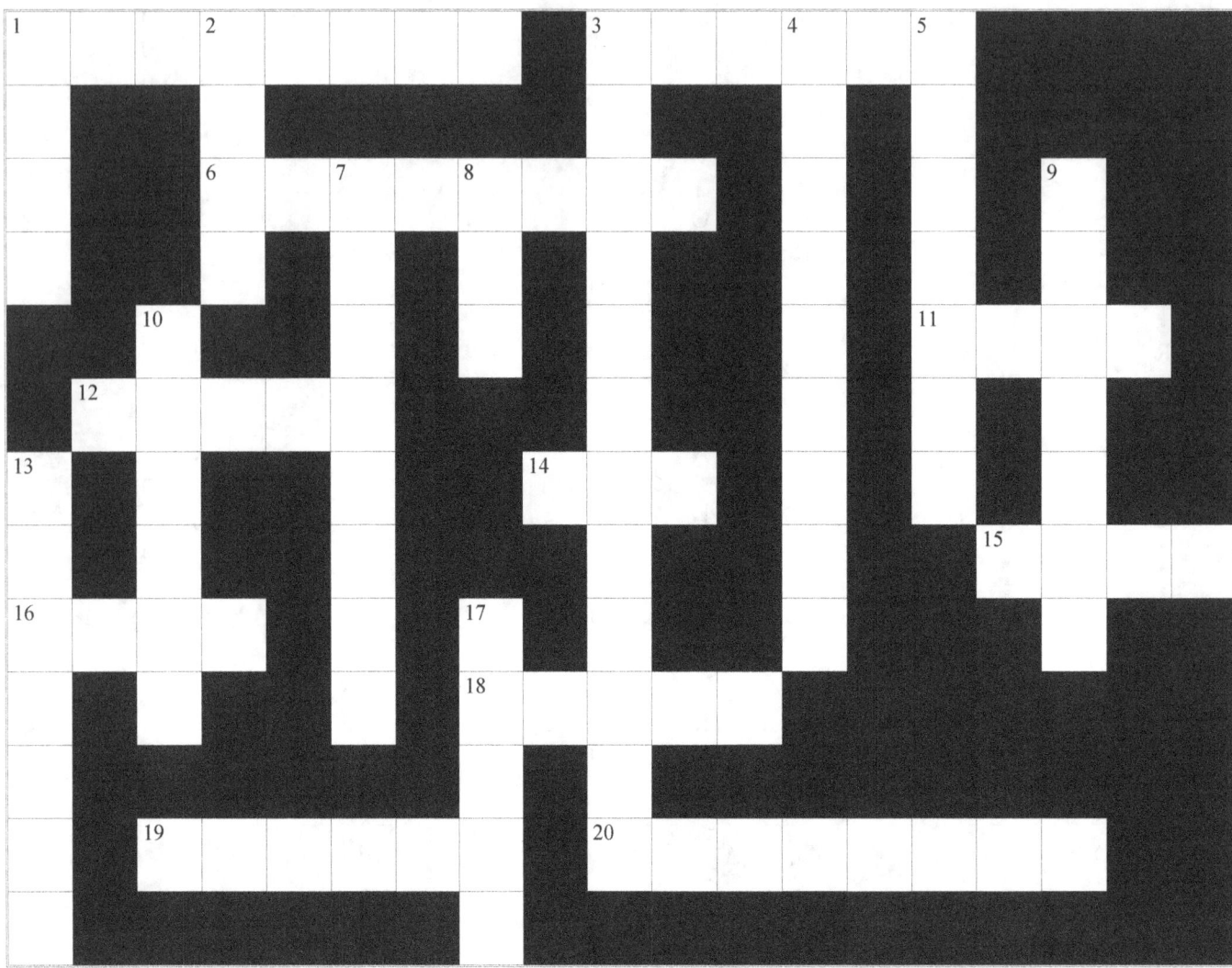

Across
1. The houses tented for ___ were being robbed.
3. Position on the soccer team Paul has always played in the past
6. Paul rats out the Tangerine soccer players for vandalizing an exhibit at the ___.
11. His older brother gets all the attention of his parents.
12. Girl who likes Paul
14. Tangerine's teams are known as the ___ Eagles.
15. Transfers to Tangerine Middle School and hates it
16. Luis hurts his leg permanently from falling out of one.
18. Theresa, Tino, and ___ all work with Paul on a school project.
19. Paul prepares a statement for the ___ explaining what he witnessed.
20. Does severe damage to Lake Windsor Middle School

Down
1. Starts a fight with Joey over a comment he made about Luis
2. This type of fire is continuously burning behind Paul's house.
3. Paul's are not interested in Erik's football achievements and plans.
4. Kills Mike Castello
5. Paul tells people he looked at an ___ for too long, causing damage to his eyes.
7. How Paul says he would feel if his brother died
8. Prevents Paul from playing soccer at LWD; later "disappears"
9. Former home of the Fisher family
10. Paul and Joey act as ___ during the sinkhole disaster.
13. Person who pulls the ball away from Erik as he goes to kick for a last minute play
17. Joey tries to take these off of his brother.

ANSWER KEY CROSSWORD - Tangerine

Across
1. The houses tented for ___ were being robbed.
3. Position on the soccer team Paul has always played in the past
6. Paul rats out the Tangerine soccer players for vandalizing an exhibit at the ___.
11. His older brother gets all the attention of his parents.
12. Girl who likes Paul
14. Tangerine's teams are known as the ___ Eagles.
15. Transfers to Tangerine Middle School and hates it
16. Luis hurts his leg permanently from falling out of one.
18. Theresa, Tino, and ___ all work with Paul on a school project.
19. Paul prepares a statement for the ___ explaining what he witnessed.
20. Does severe damage to Lake Windsor Middle School

Down
1. Starts a fight with Joey over a comment he made about Luis
2. This type of fire is continuously burning behind Paul's house.
3. Paul's are not interested in Erik's football achievements and plans.
4. Kills Mike Castello
5. Paul tells people he looked at an ___ for too long, causing damage to his eyes.
7. How Paul says he would feel if his brother died
8. Prevents Paul from playing soccer at LWD; later "disappears"
9. Former home of the Fisher family
10. Paul and Joey act as ___ during the sinkhole disaster.
13. Person who pulls the ball away from Erik as he goes to kick for a last minute play
17. Joey tries to take these off of his brother.

MATCHING 1 *Tangerine*

____ 1. EXPELLED   A. Joey tries to take these off of his brother.

____ 2. FISHER   B. Coach who participated in the Olympics for track and field

____ 3. MORNING   C. Luis creates a tangerine called the Golden ___.

____ 4. SHOES   D. Paul's are not interested in the Erik Fisher Football Dream.

____ 5. SINKHOLE   E. Position on the soccer team Paul has always played in the past

____ 6. KERRI   F. Paul's mom wants practice moved to this time of day.

____ 7. GOALIE   G. State where Paul and his family move at the start of the novel

____ 8. GOGGLES   H. Paul gets ___ from school for his actions at the award ceremony.

____ 9. LIGHTNING   I. Shows Paul around school on the first day

____ 10. CARNIVAL   J. Tangerine's teams are known as the ___ Eagles.

____ 11. THERESA   K. Does severe damage to Lake Windsor Middle School

____ 12. HENRY   L. Girl who likes Paul

____ 13. GRANDPARENTS   M. Theresa, Tino, and ___ all work with Paul on a school project.

____ 14. TERMITES   N. Starts a fight with Joey over a comment he made about Luis

____ 15. TINO   O. The houses tented for ___ were being robbed.

____ 16. ANEURYSM   P. Cause of Luis's death

____ 17. DAWN   Q. Paul's nickname at Tangerine

____ 18. WAR   R. Paul rats out the Tangerine soccer players for vandalizing an exhibit at the ___.

____ 19. BRIGHT   S. Paul wears these on his eyes while playing soccer.

____ 20. FLORIDA   T. Kills Mike Castello

MATCHING 1 ANSWER KEY *Tangerine*

H	1.	EXPELLED	A.	Joey tries to take these off of his brother.
Q	2.	FISHER	B.	Coach who participated in the Olympics for track and field
F	3.	MORNING	C.	Luis creates a tangerine called the Golden ___.
A	4.	SHOES	D.	Paul's are not interested in the Erik Fisher Football Dream.
K	5.	SINKHOLE	E.	Position on the soccer team Paul has always played in the past
L	6.	KERRI	F.	Paul's mom wants practice moved to this time of day.
E	7.	GOALIE	G.	State where Paul and his family move at the start of the novel
S	8.	GOGGLES	H.	Paul gets ___ from school for his actions at the award ceremony.
T	9.	LIGHTNING	I.	Shows Paul around school on the first day
R	10.	CARNIVAL	J.	Tangerine's teams are known as the ___ Eagles.
I	11.	THERESA	K.	Does severe damage to Lake Windsor Middle School
M	12.	HENRY	L.	Girl who likes Paul
D	13.	GRANDPARENTS	M.	Theresa, Tino, and ___ all work with Paul on a school project.
O	14.	TERMITES	N.	Starts a fight with Joey over a comment he made about Luis
N	15.	TINO	O.	The houses tented for ___ were being robbed.
P	16.	ANEURYSM	P.	Cause of Luis's death
C	17.	DAWN	Q.	Paul's nickname at Tangerine
J	18.	WAR	R.	Paul rats out the Tangerine soccer players for vandalizing an exhibit at the ___.
B	19.	BRIGHT	S.	Paul wears these on his eyes while playing soccer.
G	20.	FLORIDA	T.	Kills Mike Castello

MATCHING 2 *Tangerine*

____ 1.   RELIEVED   A. Paul thinks his dad saw Erik ___ Tino but did nothing.

____ 2.   IEP   B. Luis hurts his leg permanently from falling out of one.

____ 3.   MARS   C. Cause the coy in the pond to disappear

____ 4.   ARTHUR   D. This type of fire is continuously burning behind Paul's house.

____ 5.   BUS   E. Person who pulls the ball away from Erik as he goes to kick for a last minute play

____ 6.   THREE   F. How Paul says he would feel if his brother died

____ 7.   ECLIPSE   G. Arthur uses it to hit Luis.

____ 8.   MUD   H. Paul's nickname at Lake Windsor Downs

____ 9.   OSPREYS   I. Number of times lightning has struck Mr. Donnelly's house

____ 10. HEROES   J. Being on the ___ at Lake Windsor means you get to play the away games.

____ 11. GIRLS   K. Paul and Joey act as ___ during the sinkhole disaster.

____ 12. PUNCH   L. Antoine's little sister who plays on Paul's soccer team

____ 13. SHANDRA   M. Paul & his mom are shocked to see *they* play on the soccer team.

____ 14. SCHOLARSHIP   N. Paul finds a file on his dad's computer about Erik's ___ offers.

____ 15. MOSQUITOES   O. Side effect of soaking the fields in water to get rid of the fires

____ 16. BLACKJACK   P. Paul tells people he looked at an ___ for too long, causing damage to his eyes

____ 17. TREE   Q. Someone smears this in Paul's face, causing him to start a fight.

____ 18. ANTOINE   R. Prevents Paul from playing soccer at LWD; later "disappears"

____ 19. JOEY   S. Transfers to Tangerine Middle School & hates it

____ 20. MUCK   T. Erik's sidekick

MATCHING 2 ANSWER KEY *Tangerine*

F	1.	RELIEVED	A.	Paul thinks his dad saw Erik ___ Tino but did nothing.
R	2.	IEP	B.	Luis hurts his leg permanently from falling out of one.
H	3.	MARS	C.	Cause the coy in the pond to disappear
T	4.	ARTHUR	D.	This type of fire is continuously burning behind Paul's house.
J	5.	BUS	E.	Person who pulls the ball away from Erik as he goes to kick for a last minute play
I	6.	THREE	F.	How Paul says he would feel if his brother died
P	7.	ECLIPSE	G.	Arthur uses it to hit Luis.
Q	8.	MUD	H.	Paul's nickname at Lake Windsor Downs
C	9.	OSPREYS	I.	Number of times lightning has struck Mr. Donnelly's house
K	10.	HEROES	J.	Being on the ___ at Lake Windsor means you get to play the away games.
M	11.	GIRLS	K.	Paul and Joey act as ___ during the sinkhole disaster.
A	12.	PUNCH	L.	Antoine's little sister who plays on Paul's soccer team
L	13.	SHANDRA	M.	Paul & his mom are shocked to see *they* play on the soccer team.
N	14.	SCHOLARSHIP	N.	Paul finds a file on his dad's computer about Erik's ___ offers.
O	15.	MOSQUITOES	O.	Side effect of soaking the fields in water to get rid of the fires
G	16.	BLACKJACK	P.	Paul tells people he looked at an ___ for too long, causing damage to his eyes
B	17.	TREE	Q.	Someone smears this in Paul's face, causing him to start a fight.
E	18.	ANTOINE	R.	Prevents Paul from playing soccer at LWD; later "disappears"
S	19.	JOEY	S.	Transfers to Tangerine Middle School & hates it
D	20.	MUCK	T.	Erik's sidekick

JUGGLE LETTERS 1 *Tangerine*

_____ = 1. ALBOLOFT
The Erik Fisher ___ Dream

_____ = 2. CJKACKBAL
Arthur uses it to hit Luis.

_____ = 3. ENRUYASM
Cause of Luis's death

_____ = 4. ENANOIT
Person who pulls the ball away from Erik as he goes to kick for a last minute play

_____ = 5. YEJO
Transfers to Tangerine Middle School & hates it

_____ = 6. AICLANRV
Paul rats out the Tangerine soccer players for vandalizing an exhibit at the ___.

_____ = 7. IRHESF
Paul's nickname at Tangerine

_____ = 8. MRAS
Paul's nickname at Lake Windsor Downs

_____ = 9. RHRATU
Erik's sidekick

_____ = 10. OUEQSIOTSM
Side effect of soaking the fields in water to get rid of the fires

_____ = 11. TIESMTER
The houses tented for ___ were being robbed.

_____ = 12. FASSKBAHLC
Paul occasionally has these, about the past.

_____ = 13. DEERVELI
How Paul says he would feel if his brother died

_____ = 14. OHTONSU
Former home of the Fisher family

_____ = 15. ELLIUFINS
The county ___ all LW victories in which Antoine played.

_____ = 16. ELEPDLXE
Paul gets ___ from school for his actions at the award ceremony.

_____ = 17. NYREH
Theresa, Tino, and ___ all work with Paul on a school project.

_____ = 18. DATSRNNAPEGR
Paul's are not interested in the Erik Fisher Football Dream.

_____ = 19. LPRHAIHSSCO
Paul finds a file on his dad's computer about Erik's ___ offers.

_____ = 20. RKERI
Girl who likes Paul

JUGGLE LETTERS 1 ANSWER KEY *Tangerine*

FOOTBALL	= 1.	ALBOLOFT
		The Erik Fisher ___ Dream
BLACKJACK	= 2.	CJKACKBAL
		Arthur uses it to hit Luis.
ANEURYSM	= 3.	ENRUYASM
		Cause of Luis's death
ANTOINE	= 4.	ENANOIT
		Person who pulls the ball away from Erik as he goes to kick for a last minute play
JOEY	= 5.	YEJO
		Transfers to Tangerine Middle School & hates it
CARNIVAL	= 6.	AICLANRV
		Paul rats out the Tangerine soccer players for vandalizing an exhibit at the ___.
FISHER	= 7.	IRHESF
		Paul's nickname at Tangerine
MARS	= 8.	MRAS
		Paul's nickname at Lake Windsor Downs
ARTHUR	= 9.	RHRATU
		Erik's sidekick
MOSQUITOES	= 10.	OUEQSIOTSM
		Side effect of soaking the fields in water to get rid of the fires
TERMITES	= 11.	TIESMTER
		The houses tented for ___ were being robbed.
FLASHBACKS	= 12.	FASSKBAHLC
		Paul occasionally has these, about the past.
RELIEVED	= 13.	DEERVELI
		How Paul says he would feel if his brother died
HOUSTON	= 14.	OHTONSU
		Former home of the Fisher family
NULLIFIES	= 15.	ELLIUFINS
		The county ___ all LW victories in which Antoine played.
EXPELLED	= 16.	ELEPDLXE
		Paul gets ___ from school for his actions at the award ceremony.
HENRY	= 17.	NYREH
		Theresa, Tino, and ___ all work with Paul on a school project.
GRANDPARENTS	= 18.	DATSRNNAPEGR
		Paul's are not interested in the Erik Fisher Football Dream.
SCHOLARSHIP	= 19.	LPRHAIHSSCO
		Paul finds a file on his dad's computer about Erik's ___ offers.
KERRI	= 20.	RKERI
		Girl who likes Paul

JUGGLE LETTERS 2 *Tangerine*

_____ = 1. ASMURENY
Cause of Luis's death

_____ = 2. OGEGGLS
Paul wears these on his eyes while playing soccer.

_____ = 3. RPEYSOS
Cause the coy in the pond to disappear

_____ = 4. HIIGNNTGL
Kills Mike Castello

_____ = 5. LIRDAOF
State where Paul and his family move at the start of the novel

_____ = 6. IONT
Starts a fight with Joey over a comment he made about Luis

_____ = 7. FUANREL
Paul is asked not to attend Luis's.

_____ = 8. ELULFNIIS
The county ___ all LW victories in which Antoine played.

_____ = 9. FASHBKLASC
Paul occasionally has these, about the past.

_____ = 10. OLAIGE
Position on the soccer team Paul has always played in the past

_____ = 11. LIPEESC
Paul tells people he looked at an ___ for too long, causing damage to his eyes

_____ = 12. ENTOIAN
Person who pulls the ball away from Erik as he goes to kick for a last minute play

_____ = 13. OEJY
Transfers to Tangerine Middle School & hates it

_____ = 14. AERTESH
Shows Paul around school on the first day

_____ = 15. HFIRES
Paul's nickname at Tangerine

_____ = 16. MGONNRI
Paul's mom wants practice moved to this time of day.

_____ = 17. RHRAUT
Erik's sidekick

_____ = 18. OSNHKIEL
Does severe damage to Lake Windsor Middle School

_____ = 19. IERRK
Girl who likes Paul

_____ = 20. OCCSRE
Paul's sport

JUGGLE LETTERS 2 ANSWER KEY *Tangerine*

ANEURYSM	= 1.	ASMURENY Cause of Luis's death
GOGGLES	= 2.	OGEGGLS Paul wears these on his eyes while playing soccer.
OSPREYS	= 3.	RPEYSOS Cause the coy in the pond to disappear
LIGHTNING	= 4.	HIIGNNTGL Kills Mike Castello
FLORIDA	= 5.	LIRDAOF State where Paul and his family move at the start of the novel
TINO	= 6.	IONT Starts a fight with Joey over a comment he made about Luis
FUNERAL	= 7.	FUANREL Paul is asked not to attend Luis's.
NULLIFIES	= 8.	ELULFNIIS The county ___ all LW victories in which Antoine played.
FLASHBACKS	= 9.	FASHBKLASC Paul occasionally has these, about the past.
GOALIE	= 10.	OLAIGE Position on the soccer team Paul has always played in the past
ECLIPSE	= 11.	LIPEESC Paul tells people he looked at an ___ for too long, causing damage to his eyes
ANTOINE	= 12.	ENTOIAN Person who pulls the ball away from Erik as he goes to kick for a last minute play
JOEY	= 13.	OEJY Transfers to Tangerine Middle School & hates it
THERESA	= 14.	AERTESH Shows Paul around school on the first day
FISHER	= 15.	HFIRES Paul's nickname at Tangerine
MORNING	= 16.	MGONNRI Paul's mom wants practice moved to this time of day.
ARTHUR	= 17.	RHRAUT Erik's sidekick
SINKHOLE	= 18.	OSNHKIEL Does severe damage to Lake Windsor Middle School
KERRI	= 19.	IERRK Girl who likes Paul
SOCCER	= 20.	OCCSRE Paul's sport

VOCABULARY RESOURCE MATERIALS

Tangerine Vocabulary

No.	Word	Clue/Definition
1.	ABRUPTLY	Suddenly or unexpectedly
2.	ADJOURN	Suspend (as a meeting) to or until another place and/or time
3.	AFFIDAVITS	Written statements made under oath
4.	AGITATED	Upset or disturbed
5.	AGONIZING	Filled with distress, suffering, or torture; worrying in a distressed way
6.	ANEURYSM	A swell, almost like a bubble, in an artery resulting from the weakening of the blood vessel wall; if it bursts, it is usually fatal
7.	ARCHENEMY	Chief or main enemy
8.	ASTRIDE	One leg on either side of; straddling
9.	BANTER	Light, teasing, playful remarks
10.	BILLOWING	Moving (usually upward or outward) in a rolling, swelling motion
11.	BROODED	Was in deep thought; focused attention on a subject persistently
12.	CALISTHENICS	Exercises to develop muscles
13.	CAPSIZING	Turning or flipping over
14.	COMPREHEND	Understand
15.	CONSCIENCE	One's own moral or ethical awareness of right and wrong
16.	CONSTITUTES	Makes the elements or parts of
17.	CONTORT	Twist into a strange shape or expression
18.	CONVICTION	Fixed or firm belief
19.	CONVOY	Escort; an accompanying or protecting force; a group (as of vehicles) traveling together for convenience
20.	COOPERATED	Worked together willingly and agreeably
21.	CORRUGATED	Having folds, ridges, and grooves
22.	CUE	Signal used to prompt an action
23.	DECOY	Something or someone used to lure or mislead another into a trap
24.	DESPISED	Disliked intensely; scorned; loathed
25.	DILAPIDATED	Ruined or decayed from age, wear, or neglect
26.	DISBELIEF	Amazement or astonishment
27.	DISCLOSURE	Making facts and details evident and clear
28.	DISINFECTANT	Chemical agent used to destroy bacteria
29.	DISINTEGRATING	Breaking up; deteriorating; falling apart
30.	DWELL	Focus one's attention on (usually a thought) for an extended time
31.	ECLIPSE	The disappearance of the whole or a part of the sun when the moon comes between it and earth, or of the moon when the earth's shadow falls upon it
32.	ELATED	Very happy or proud; in high spirits

No.	Word	Clue/Definition
33.	EXPLOITS	Outstanding events in which a person puts his/her strong points to the best advantage
34.	FORFEIT	Surrender or give up as punishment for a crime, error, or offense
35.	FUMIGATED	Subjected to smoke or fumes, usually to exterminate bugs
36.	GHOULISH	Strangely cruel or monstrous
37.	GNAT	Very small, biting fly
38.	HASTILY	Quickly
39.	HEAVE	Rise up or swell; bulge; lift
40.	HORTICULTURE	The science or art of cultivating plants
41.	IMPATIENT	Wanting to hurry up; not wanting to wait for something to be done or to happen
42.	INCONSISTENT	Not regular or predictable
43.	INFRACTION	Violation; breach
44.	INSOLENTLY	In a way that is boldly rude or disrespectful
45.	INTENTLY	With great concentration or eager attention
46.	INTERVENED	Came between to mediate or help
47.	IRREGULARITIES	Things that are not within the usual rules or customs
48.	JEERING	Mocking, taunting, or verbally abusing
49.	JITTERY	Extremely tense or nervous
50.	LIABLE	Legally obligated or responsible
51.	MENACING	Threatening or dangerous
52.	MESMERIZED	Spellbound; enthralled; hypnotized
53.	NULLIFY	Declare something void; invalidate
54.	OBLIGED	Required; bonded
55.	OMINOUSLY	In a threatening way
56.	OVATION	Enthusiastic, prolonged applause
57.	PARALLEL	Extending in the same direction, equally distant at every point
58.	PELTING	Bombarding; striking rapidly and repeatedly
59.	PERIMETER	Border or boundary
60.	PERSISTENT	Refuses to give up or let go; long-lasting
61.	PRIED	Separated or moved something with great difficulty
62.	PROMINENCE	The condition of being immediately noticeable or recognizable; being outstanding or well-known
63.	PROSTRATE	Lying flat on the ground in humility or submission; helpless
64.	RECEDING	Becoming more distant
65.	RELENTLESSLY	Steadily; in a way never giving up
66.	RELUCTANTLY	Not willingly; with resistance or hesitation
67.	RESEMBLANCE	Similarity of likeness with something else
68.	RESTITUTION	Compensation for loss or damage
69.	RETALIATE	Get revenge; pay back in kind for a wrong-doing

No.	Word	Clue/Definition
70.	REVERENCE	Feeling or attitude of deep respect
71.	RIGID	Stiff; inflexible; hard
72.	ROUT	An overwhelming defeat
73.	SATURATING	Soaking thoroughly and completely
74.	SCARCE	Uncommonly or infrequently found or seen
75.	SCRIMMAGE	Practice session or informal game
76.	SINGED	Burned slightly; scorched
77.	SOLEMNLY	Seriously; gravely; in a somber manner
78.	SPECTACLE	Public performance or display
79.	SUBDUED	Quiet; repressed; controlled
80.	TROUNCED	Beat severely
81.	UNISON	Corresponding exactly and occurring simultaneously
82.	UNPRECEDENTED	Never before known, experienced, or done
83.	VEERED	Turned or swerved off course
84.	VEHEMENTLY	Strongly; violently; with forceful expression of emotion or belief
85.	VERGE	On the edge; the point where an action is likely to begin
86.	VICIOUS	Ferocious; unpleasantly severe
87.	VULNERABLE	Capable of being wounded or hurt
88.	WAIVE	Give up a right or claim voluntarily
89.	WRATH	Strong, vindictive, or fierce anger

VOCABULARY WORD SEARCH - Tangerine

```
U N P R E C E D E N T E D I S C L O S U R E G
D E I T L Y H E I S P V I C I O U S C P D L W
E X N D A L A C F L D A R W V E J S I R I B F
S P S E T T S O W U A I R U T K P O N O S A J
P L O N E P T Y M F M P N A C U E L E S B I T
I O L E D U I X Z M B I I T L Q G E H T E L W
S I E V O R L R A M S L G D H L X M T R L L N
E T N R J B Y G W O A T D A A Y E N S A I D T
D S T E E A E S N T Y N W S T T D L I T E L H
I G L T E C M N E L R A E V O E E Y L E F K D
R H Y N R O H R T G K T L E V W D D A N M A D
T O C I I Z M N D Y D C L H A M O S C T R C Q
S U K P N V A I F T E E P E T N O S K C Y S E
A L F J G T R I N R C F D M I N R W H L K L D
A I W Z C V L W N O N N P E O M B E V T B P K
N S F U E L A W R R U I P N N C N S D A G H S
E H L R U I S G E H O S M T M E P V R F D C Z
U E G N V Z I T N E R I L L M E G E B O A V H
R E V E R E N C E A T D D Y C O N T O R T E X
Y I C K D A G L R V T E O T X L I A C F P E W
S L G X B T E Z J E I V A J U P T E C E X R Z
M J J I M Y D Z L R N C Q V S N L K R I A E J
T S U B D U E D P O L O B L I G E D L T N D M
I N T E N T L Y C E C L I P S E P J H X H G X
```

ABRUPTLY	FUMIGATED	REVERENCE
ANEURYSM	GHOULISH	RIGID
ARCHENEMY	GNAT	ROUT
ASTRIDE	HASTILY	SCARCE
BANTER	HEAVE	SCRIMMAGE
BROODED	INSOLENTLY	SINGED
CALISTHENICS	INTENTLY	SOLEMNLY
CONTORT	INTERVENED	SPECTACLE
CONVOY	JEERING	SUBDUED
CUE	LIABLE	TROUNCED
DECOY	MENACING	UNISON
DESPISED	NULLIFY	UNPRECEDENTED
DILAPIDATED	OBLIGED	VEERED
DISBELIEF	OMINOUSLY	VEHEMENTLY
DISCLOSURE	OVATION	VERGE
DISINFECTANT	PARALLEL	VICIOUS
DWELL	PELTING	VULNERABLE
ECLIPSE	PRIED	WAIVE
ELATED	PROSTRATE	WRATH
EXPLOITS	RELUCTANTLY	
FORFEIT	RETALIATE	

ANSWER KEY VOCABULARY WORD SEARCH - Tangerine

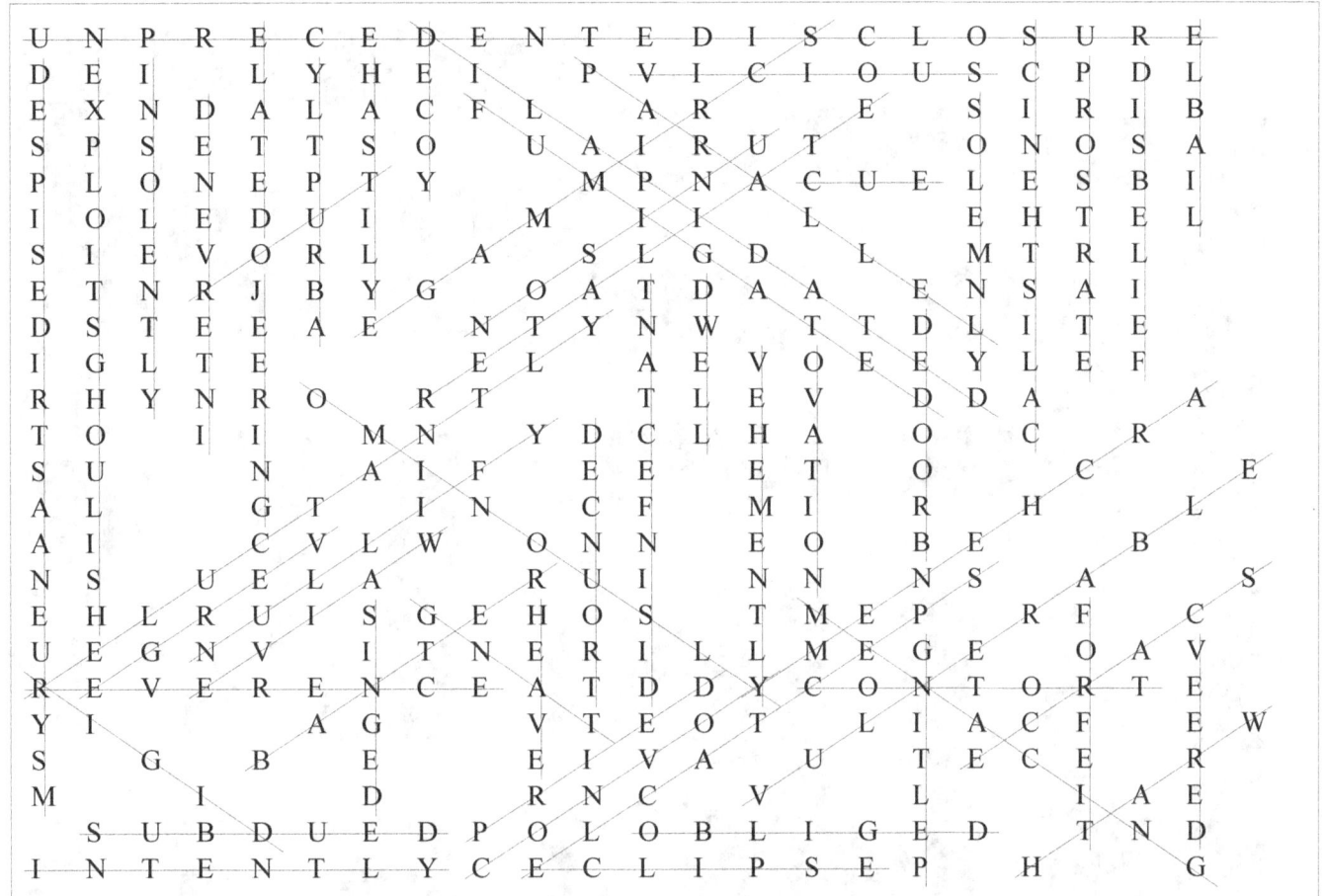

ABRUPTLY	FUMIGATED	REVERENCE
ANEURYSM	GHOULISH	RIGID
ARCHENEMY	GNAT	ROUT
ASTRIDE	HASTILY	SCARCE
BANTER	HEAVE	SCRIMMAGE
BROODED	INSOLENTLY	SINGED
CALISTHENICS	INTENTLY	SOLEMNLY
CONTORT	INTERVENED	SPECTACLE
CONVOY	JEERING	SUBDUED
CUE	LIABLE	TROUNCED
DECOY	MENACING	UNISON
DESPISED	NULLIFY	UNPRECEDENTED
DILAPIDATED	OBLIGED	VEERED
DISBELIEF	OMINOUSLY	VEHEMENTLY
DISCLOSURE	OVATION	VERGE
DISINFECTANT	PARALLEL	VICIOUS
DWELL	PELTING	VULNERABLE
ECLIPSE	PRIED	WAIVE
ELATED	PROSTRATE	WRATH
EXPLOITS	RELUCTANTLY	
FORFEIT	RETALIATE	

VOCABULARY CROSSWORD - Tangerine

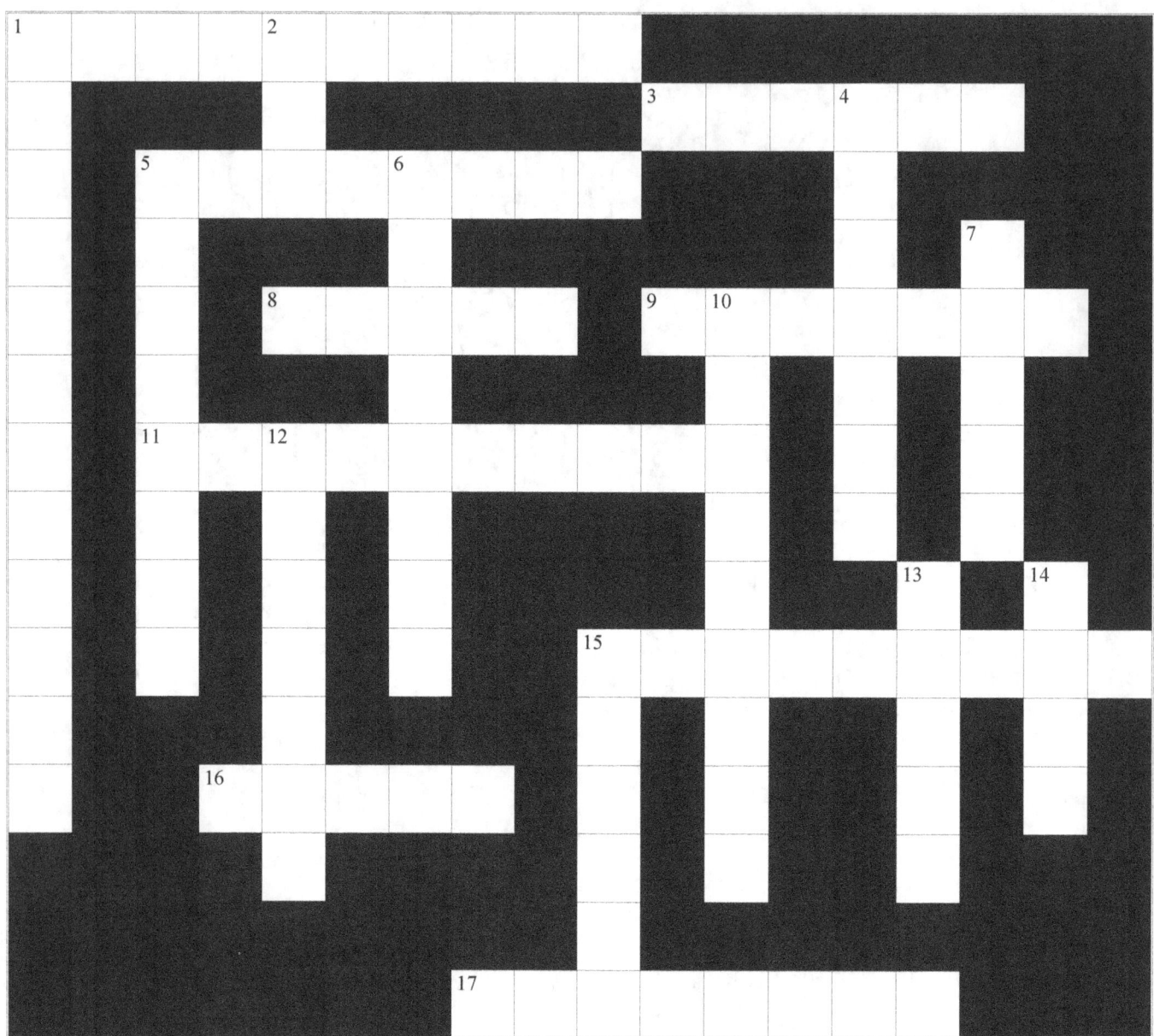

Across
1. One's own moral or ethical awareness of right and wrong
3. Legally obligated or responsible
5. A swell, almost like a bubble, in an artery; if it bursts, it is usually fatal
8. Something or someone used to lure or mislead another into a trap
9. Suspend (as a meeting) to or until another place or time
11. Written statements made under oath
15. Moving (usually upward or outward) in a rolling, swelling motion
16. Stiff; inflexible; hard
17. Suddenly or unexpectedly

Down
1. Exercises to develop muscles
2. Signal used to prompt an action
4. Was in deep thought; focused attention on one subject persistently
5. Upset or disturbed
6. Becoming more distant
7. Separated or moved something with great difficulty
10. Amazement or astonishment
12. Surrender or give up as punishment for a crime, error, or offense
13. Focus one's attention on (usually a thought) for an extended period of time
14. Very small, biting fly
15. Light, teasing, playful remarks

ANSWER KEY VOCABULARY CROSSWORD - Tangerine

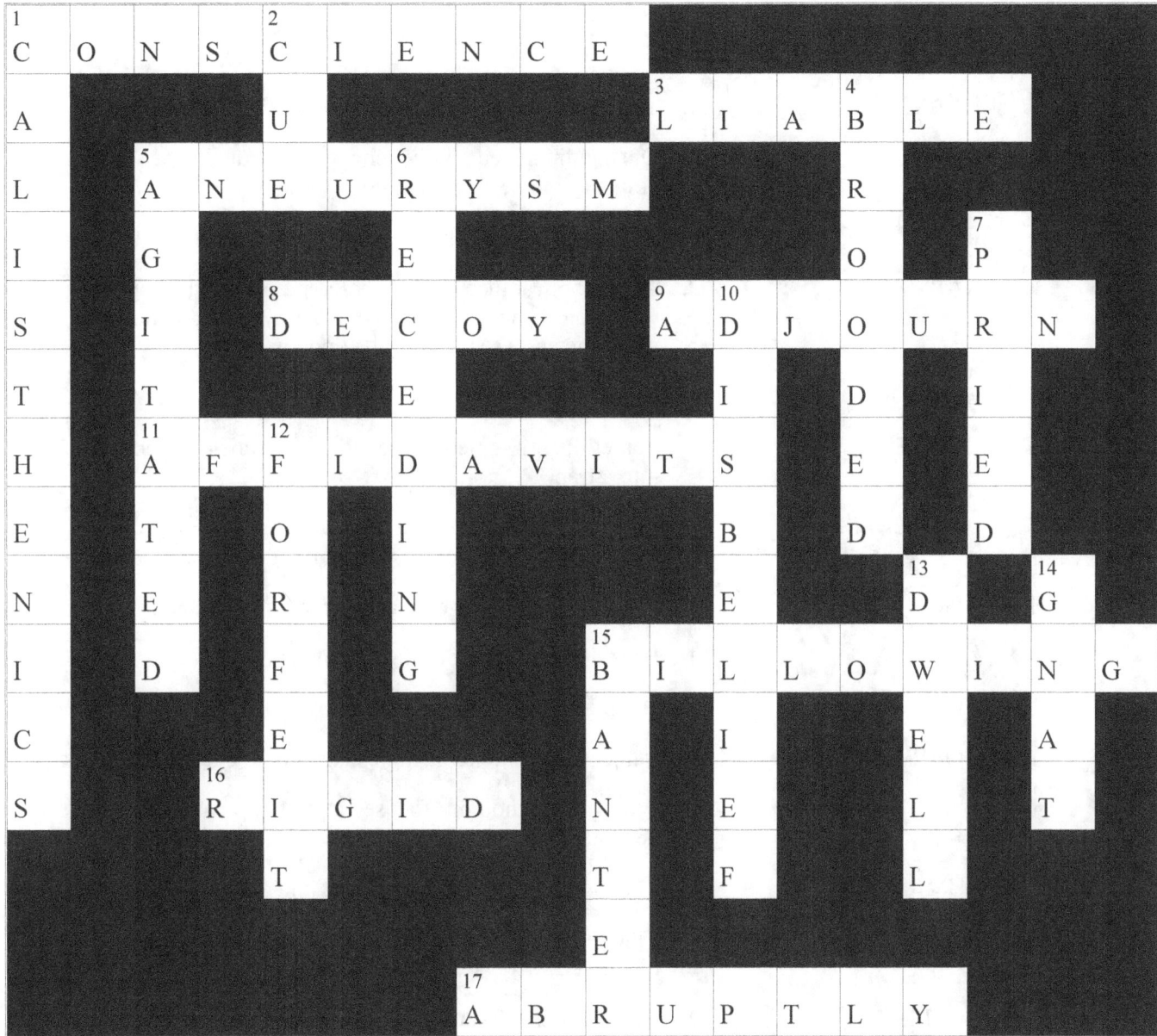

Across
1. One's own moral or ethical awareness of right and wrong
3. Legally obligated or responsible
5. A swell, almost like a bubble, in an artery; if it bursts, it is usually fatal
8. Something or someone used to lure or mislead another into a trap
9. Suspend (as a meeting) to or until another place or time
11. Written statements made under oath
15. Moving (usually upward or outward) in a rolling, swelling motion
16. Stiff; inflexible; hard
17. Suddenly or unexpectedly

Down
1. Exercises to develop muscles
2. Signal used to prompt an action
4. Was in deep thought; focused attention on one subject persistently
5. Upset or disturbed
6. Becoming more distant
7. Separated or moved something with great difficulty
10. Amazement or astonishment
12. Surrender or give up as punishment for a crime, error, or offense
13. Focus one's attention on (usually a thought) for an extended period of time
14. Very small, biting fly
15. Light, teasing, playful remarks

VOCABULARY MATCHING 1 *Tangerine*

____ 1. HEAVE   A. Twist into a strange shape or expression

____ 2. CONTORT   B. Outstanding events in which a person puts his/her strong points to the best advantage

____ 3. CONSCIENCE   C. Very small, biting fly

____ 4. CAPSIZING   D. The disappearance of the whole or a part of the sun when the moon comes between it and earth, or of the moon when the earth's shadow falls upon it

____ 5. BROODED   E. Turning or flipping over

____ 6. BANTER   F. Something or someone used to lure or mislead another into a trap

____ 7. ARCHENEMY   G. Escort; an accompanying or protecting force; a group (as of vehicles) traveling together for convenience

____ 8. AGONIZING   H. One's own moral or ethical awareness of right and wrong

____ 9. AFFIDAVITS   I. Breaking up; deteriorating; falling apart

____ 10. CONVOY   J. Having folds, ridges, and grooves

____ 11. CORRUGATED   K. Subjected to smoke or fumes, usually to exterminate bugs

____ 12. GNAT   L. Was in deep thought; focused attention on a subject persistently

____ 13. FUMIGATED   M. Making facts and details evident and clear

____ 14. EXPLOITS   N. Filled with distress, suffering, or torture; worrying in a distressed way

____ 15. ECLIPSE   O. Rise up or swell; bulge; lift

____ 16. DISINTEGRATING   P. Suddenly or unexpectedly

____ 17. DISCLOSURE   Q. Written statements made under oath

____ 18. DILAPIDATED   R. Light, teasing, playful remarks

____ 19. DECOY   S. Chief or main enemy

____ 20. ABRUPTLY   T. Ruined or decayed from age, wear, or neglect

VOCABULARY MATCHING 1 ANSWER KEY *Tangerine*

O	1.	HEAVE	A.	Twist into a strange shape or expression
A	2.	CONTORT	B.	Outstanding events in which a person puts his/her strong points to the best advantage
H	3.	CONSCIENCE	C.	Very small, biting fly
E	4.	CAPSIZING	D.	The disappearance of the whole or a part of the sun when the moon comes between it and earth, or of the moon when the earth's shadow falls upon it
L	5.	BROODED	E.	Turning or flipping over
R	6.	BANTER	F.	Something or someone used to lure or mislead another into a trap
S	7.	ARCHENEMY	G.	Escort; an accompanying or protecting force; a group (as of vehicles) traveling together for convenience
N	8.	AGONIZING	H.	One's own moral or ethical awareness of right and wrong
Q	9.	AFFIDAVITS	I.	Breaking up; deteriorating; falling apart
G	10.	CONVOY	J.	Having folds, ridges, and grooves
J	11.	CORRUGATED	K.	Subjected to smoke or fumes, usually to exterminate bugs
C	12.	GNAT	L.	Was in deep thought; focused attention on a subject persistently
K	13.	FUMIGATED	M.	Making facts and details evident and clear
B	14.	EXPLOITS	N.	Filled with distress, suffering, or torture; worrying in a distressed way
D	15.	ECLIPSE	O.	Rise up or swell; bulge; lift
I	16.	DISINTEGRATING	P.	Suddenly or unexpectedly
M	17.	DISCLOSURE	Q.	Written statements made under oath
T	18.	DILAPIDATED	R.	Light, teasing, playful remarks
F	19.	DECOY	S.	Chief or main enemy
P	20.	ABRUPTLY	T.	Ruined or decayed from age, wear, or neglect

VOCABULARY MATCHING 2 *Tangerine*

___ 1. WRATH A. Get revenge; pay back in kind for a wrong-doing

___ 2. RESEMBLANCE B. Spellbound; enthralled; hypnotized

___ 3. RELENTLESSLY C. Quiet; repressed; controlled

___ 4. PROSTRATE D. Corresponding exactly and occurring simultaneously

___ 5. PRIED E. Similarity of likeness with something else

___ 6. PELTING F. Practice session or informal game

___ 7. OMINOUSLY G. Seriously; gravely; in a somber manner

___ 8. MESMERIZED H. Legally obligated or responsible

___ 9. LIABLE I. Turned or swerved off course

___ 10. RETALIATE J. Things that are not within the usual rules or customs

___ 11. RIGID K. Capable of being wounded or hurt

___ 12. VULNERABLE L. On the edge; the point where an action is likely to begin

___ 13. VERGE M. Stiff; inflexible; hard

___ 14. VEERED N. In a threatening way

___ 15. UNISON O. Lying flat on the ground in humility or submission; helpless

___ 16. SUBDUED P. Bombarding; striking rapidly and repeatedly

___ 17. SOLEMNLY Q. Separated or moved something with great difficulty

___ 18. SCRIMMAGE R. Strong, vindictive, or fierce anger

___ 19. SATURATING S. Soaking thoroughly and completely

___ 20. IRREGULARITIES T. Steadily; in a way never giving up

VOCABULARY MATCHING 2 ANSWER KEY *Tangerine*

R	1.	WRATH	A.	Get revenge; pay back in kind for a wrong-doing
E	2.	RESEMBLANCE	B.	Spellbound; enthralled; hypnotized
T	3.	RELENTLESSLY	C.	Quiet; repressed; controlled
O	4.	PROSTRATE	D.	Corresponding exactly and occurring simultaneously
Q	5.	PRIED	E.	Similarity of likeness with something else
P	6.	PELTING	F.	Practice session or informal game
N	7.	OMINOUSLY	G.	Seriously; gravely; in a somber manner
B	8.	MESMERIZED	H.	Legally obligated or responsible
H	9.	LIABLE	I.	Turned or swerved off course
A	10.	RETALIATE	J.	Things that are not within the usual rules or customs
M	11.	RIGID	K.	Capable of being wounded or hurt
K	12.	VULNERABLE	L.	On the edge; the point where an action is likely to begin
L	13.	VERGE	M.	Stiff; inflexible; hard
I	14.	VEERED	N.	In a threatening way
D	15.	UNISON	O.	Lying flat on the ground in humility or submission; helpless
C	16.	SUBDUED	P.	Bombarding; striking rapidly and repeatedly
G	17.	SOLEMNLY	Q.	Separated or moved something with great difficulty
F	18.	SCRIMMAGE	R.	Strong, vindictive, or fierce anger
S	19.	SATURATING	S.	Soaking thoroughly and completely
J	20.	IRREGULARITIES	T.	Steadily; in a way never giving up

VOCABULARY JUGGLE LETTERS 1 *Tangerine*

_____ = 1. GIIRD
Stiff; inflexible; hard

_____ = 2. EODBROD
Was in deep thought; focused attention on a subject persistently

_____ = 3. ITDRESA
One leg on either side of; straddling

_____ = 4. DTVFISAAIF
Written statements made under oath

_____ = 5. UBARLYPT
Suddenly or unexpectedly

_____ = 6. CRASEC
Uncommonly or infrequently found or seen

_____ = 7. DOCURTEN
Beat severely

_____ = 8. NIOUSN
Corresponding exactly and occurring simultaneously

_____ = 9. UIICOVS
Ferocious; unpleasantly severe

_____ = 10. NDEEHOCRPM
Understand

_____ = 11. CRONTTO
Twist into a strange shape or expression

_____ = 12. IREUTOINTST
Compensation for loss or damage

_____ = 13. PRTSROETA
Lying flat on the ground in humility or submission; helpless

_____ = 14. ILMOSYOUN
In a threatening way

_____ = 15. ECNAIMGN
Threatening or dangerous

_____ = 16. HEVEA
Rise up or swell; bulge; lift

_____ = 17. FIFOTER
Surrender or give up as punishment for a crime, error, or offense

_____ = 18. SLEOTXIP
Outstanding events in which a person puts his/her strong points to the best advantage

_____ = 19. ECOYD
Something or someone used to lure or mislead another into a trap

_____ = 20. RHATW
Strong, vindictive, or fierce anger

VOCABULARY JUGGLE LETTERS 1 ANSWER KEY *Tangerine*

RIGID	= 1.	GIIRD Stiff; inflexible; hard
BROODED	= 2.	EODBROD Was in deep thought; focused attention on a subject persistently
ASTRIDE	= 3.	ITDRESA One leg on either side of; straddling
AFFIDAVITS	= 4.	DTVFISAAIF Written statements made under oath
ABRUPTLY	= 5.	UBARLYPT Suddenly or unexpectedly
SCARCE	= 6.	CRASEC Uncommonly or infrequently found or seen
TROUNCED	= 7.	DOCURTEN Beat severely
UNISON	= 8.	NIOUSN Corresponding exactly and occurring simultaneously
VICIOUS	= 9.	UIICOVS Ferocious; unpleasantly severe
COMPREHEND	= 10.	NDEEHOCRPM Understand
CONTORT	= 11.	CRONTTO Twist into a strange shape or expression
RESTITUTION	= 12.	IREUTOINTST Compensation for loss or damage
PROSTRATE	= 13.	PRTSROETA Lying flat on the ground in humility or submission; helpless
OMINOUSLY	= 14.	ILMOSYOUN In a threatening way
MENACING	= 15.	ECNAIMGN Threatening or dangerous
HEAVE	= 16.	HEVEA Rise up or swell; bulge; lift
FORFEIT	= 17.	FIFOTER Surrender or give up as punishment for a crime, error, or offense
EXPLOITS	= 18.	SLEOTXIP Outstanding events in which a person puts his/her strong points to the best advantage
DECOY	= 19.	ECOYD Something or someone used to lure or mislead another into a trap
WRATH	= 20.	RHATW Strong, vindictive, or fierce anger

VOCABULARY JUGGLE LETTERS 2 *Tangerine*

_____ = 1. STPTINESER
Refuses to give up or let go; long-lasting

_____ = 2. SAIILCHNCTSE
Exercises to develop muscles

_____ = 3. NBTERA
Light, teasing, playful remarks

_____ = 4. AAEGTIDT
Upset or disturbed

_____ = 5. JRUOAND
Suspend (as a meeting) to or until another place and/or time

_____ = 6. ARBECESLMNE
Similarity of likeness with something else

_____ = 7. IGDIR
Stiff; inflexible; hard

_____ = 8. ELCCPEATS
Public performance or display

_____ = 9. TEPEECNDDRNEU
Never before known, experienced, or done

_____ = 10. SNCNIECECO
One's own moral or ethical awareness of right and wrong

_____ = 11. OECARPEODT
Worked together willingly and agreeably

_____ = 12. OTOANVI
Enthusiastic, prolonged applause

_____ = 13. FLNUYIL
Declare something void; invalidate

_____ = 14. ALBEIL
Legally obligated or responsible

_____ = 15. EGIIASRLURITER
Things that are not within the usual rules or customs

_____ = 16. ELRUHRTCITOU
The science or art of cultivating plants

_____ = 17. GIULHSHO
Strangely cruel or monstrous

_____ = 18. ELDATE
Very happy or proud; in high spirits

_____ = 19. AIIPADTDDEL
Ruined or decayed from age, wear, or neglect

_____ = 20. IWVAE
Give up a right or claim voluntarily

VOCABULARY JUGGLE LETTERS 2 ANSWER KEY *Tangerine*

PERSISTENT	= 1.	STPTINESER Refuses to give up or let go; long-lasting
CALISTHENICS	= 2.	SAIILCHNCTSE Exercises to develop muscles
BANTER	= 3.	NBTERA Light, teasing, playful remarks
AGITATED	= 4.	AAEGTIDT Upset or disturbed
ADJOURN	= 5.	JRUOAND Suspend (as a meeting) to or until another place and/or time
RESEMBLANCE	= 6.	ARBECESLMNE Similarity of likeness with something else
RIGID	= 7.	IGDIR Stiff; inflexible; hard
SPECTACLE	= 8.	ELCCPEATS Public performance or display
UNPRECEDENTED	= 9.	TEPEECNDDRNEU Never before known, experienced, or done
CONSCIENCE	= 10.	SNCNIECECO One's own moral or ethical awareness of right and wrong
COOPERATED	= 11.	OECARPEODT Worked together willingly and agreeably
OVATION	= 12.	OTOANVI Enthusiastic, prolonged applause
NULLIFY	= 13.	FLNUYIL Declare something void; invalidate
LIABLE	= 14.	ALBEIL Legally obligated or responsible
IRREGULARITIES	= 15.	EGIIASRLURITER Things that are not within the usual rules or customs
HORTICULTURE	= 16.	ELRUHRTCITOU The science or art of cultivating plants
GHOULISH	= 17.	GIULHSHO Strangely cruel or monstrous
ELATED	= 18.	ELDATE Very happy or proud; in high spirits
DILAPIDATED	= 19.	AIIPADTDDEL Ruined or decayed from age, wear, or neglect
WAIVE	= 20.	IWVAE Give up a right or claim voluntarily

www.ingramcontent.com/pod-product-compliance
Lightning Source LLC
Chambersburg PA
CBHW051403070526
44584CB00023B/3279